Plate 82.

The Damask Rose   1. Flower   Rosa Damascena

Eliz. Blackwell delin. sculp. et Pinx.   2. Bud

The Side Gardener

The

SIDE
GARDENER

Recipes & Notes from My Garden

BY

Rosie Daykin

PHOTOGRAPHY BY

Andrew Montgomery

appetite

by RANDOM HOUSE

Appetite by Random House® and colophon are registered trademarks of Penguin Random House LLC.

Library and Archives Canada Cataloguing in Publication is available upon request.
ISBN: 978-0-525-61217-9
eBook ISBN: 978-0-525-61218-6

Photography: Andrew Montgomery
Cover and book design: Kelly Hill
Map on page 10: Wendy Nooney
Endpaper images: George Arents Collection, The New York Public Library.
"Peas" The New York Public Library Digital Collections. 1751.
https://digitalcollections.nypl.org/items/09b7acf0-fcde-0136-b64d-0819a9ad2c1f;
"The damask rose" The New York Public Library Digital Collections. 1751.
https://digitalcollections.nypl.org/items/096ac960-fcde-0136-d66b-0013d294478a;
"Columbine" The New York Public Library Digital Collections. 1739.
https://digitalcollections.nypl.org/items/358134f0-6da6-0136-522f-3daa98b5be19;
"Garden cucumber" The New York Public Library Digital Collections. 1751.
https://digitalcollections.nypl.org/items/ec3f0ba0-fcdd-0136-e197-0c7e27bce827

Printed in China

Published in Canada by Appetite by Random House®,
a division of Penguin Random House Canada Limited.

www.penguinrandomhouse.ca

10 9 8 7 6 5 4 3 2 1

appetite
by RANDOM HOUSE   Penguin
Random House
Canada

For hope and possibility,
the foundation of every garden

CONTENTS

THE CHICKENS

THE FLOWERS

INTRODUCTION

Like so many of us, I had more than a few sleepless nights at the beginning of the pandemic. I would lie in the dark fretting over the future, the safety of my loved ones, and the precarious state we now found ourselves living in.

Historically when faced with a challenge, I have relied upon my theory that answers are lighter than issues. I like to believe that if I lie still enough in the dark with a quiet mind, the solutions I am seeking will slowly float to the surface, revealing themselves like little bubbles in a glass of champagne. I can't tell you where or when I learned that if you are trying to prevent a landslide, you need to plant vegetation to help retain the soil. But clearly that little nugget was lodged somewhere deep inside my brain, for just as the ground was starting to slip out from beneath my feet, instinct told me to grab some seeds and a shovel.

Although creating our side garden wasn't a new idea, it finally felt like the right time. My husband, Paul, and I had been wanting to tackle this project for several years but somehow, between work, travel, and the demands of everyday life, the opportunity never arose. Perhaps every dark cloud really does have a silver lining. Building the garden would give us the much-needed distraction and focus we craved, and provide a goal to work toward while we waited out lockdown. It was a small piece of our world we could control.

Our side yard is a funny spot that few are even aware exists. You can't see it from any vantage point other than its actual entrance. With its southern exposure and protected position, it was an ideal spot for a garden, but any efforts in the past to use it proved unsuccessful because we'd always forget to water. As they say, "out of sight, out of mind." Ultimately our forgetfulness would be remedied with an irrigation system, but not before a lot of other steps.

Paul and I measured the space and agreed upon a layout of raised planters on a bed of fine pea gravel, just as we'd seen many times throughout our travels in England and France. If the pandemic was going to keep us home, at least we still had the memories of so many other wonderful gardens to draw inspiration from while we built ours.

I felt confident that my choice of using few but consistent elements would create the space I desired. Varying shades of gray in a variety of materials would ultimately act as the perfect backdrop for the bounty of vegetables and flowers that I hoped would one day fill it.

I made some calls. As luck would have it, Lou, the fence guy, was available. As was Leon, the handyman, and Aaron, the painter. All of them were happy to take on a project that allowed them to work outdoors independently while still abiding by the necessary restrictions. Bit by bit, the structure of the garden started to come together. I'd be lying if I said it wasn't a lot of work, but something amazing was developing there. Upon entering the garden, all the stress and worry brought on by the state of our new normal would magically start to dissipate.

Even the grueling act of shoveling buckets of pea gravel or lugging endless bags of dirt somehow became tranquil and relaxing. Paul might argue this, given that the division of labor wasn't always equal, but both of us agree the creation of the side garden was one of the most rewarding projects we've ever taken on. Believe me, after thirty-five years of marriage and nine different homes, we've had our fair share. While I encourage gardening with your spouse, I highly recommend you avoid wallpapering or assembling anything from IKEA.

Deciding what vegetables to plant involved a bit of trial and error, which is how I've learned to do just about everything in life. I was a self-taught interior designer for years before deciding in 2007 to open a bakery, with no training. I've always preferred to jump into things feet first and figure it out along the way. Fortunately, seeds and starter vegetable plants are relatively inexpensive, so my education wasn't too costly. I'm grateful to also know some very talented gardeners who were, and continue to be, patient and helpful when I seek their advice. As a result, much of the garden was a huge success with very little effort. A simple sprinkle of seeds produced wee shoots within days for crunchy French radishes; heads of tender butter lettuce appeared, as did an endless supply of zucchini and their delicious blossoms, spicy peppers, and all the fresh herbs I could have ever wished for.

Other plantings sadly suffered a different fate. Our tomatoes endured a very wet May and developed powdery mildew there was no coming back from; as disappointing as this was, it taught me a valuable lesson about planting too early and overcrowding the beds. Then there was something odd that happened to my lemon cucumber that I still can't explain, and I gave up on the fennel after I realized I had mistakenly planted the herb variety, which gave me nothing but 4 feet of frothy tops and no bulbs. So you see: a little trial, a little error, and many lessons learned along the way.

I've always said I can't imagine a home without flowers, and that goes doubly for a garden. Back in 2006 when we first renovated our house, I designed the gardens with a more contemporary style to reflect the interiors. I went with low-maintenance plants and ground cover like bamboo, boxwood, ferns, salal, and ornamental grasses. The few roses I attempted to grow were an abysmal failure. At the time life was hectic with raising our daughter and running my bakery, which resulted in a serious lack of attention and the roses' ensuing death. Given our history, Paul and I accepted that an irrigation system would be essential to our new garden's survival. The immediate relief it provided is akin to that first time we opted to use the navigation system in a rental car. Without question, it was one of the most peaceful drives we've ever taken with no finger pointing, no cursing, and no wrong turns. I like to imagine that same woman with the monotone voice who wisely guided us through the Italian countryside is now watering our vegetable beds and flower pots every morning at 6:15.

Flowers I had been purchasing for years to fill my home were now able to happily grow in our garden, free for the cutting. The climbing roses I longed for in beautiful shades of soft pink and peach were slowly but surely making their way across the wall of lattice, thrilled with the afternoon heat it radiated. Whimsical dahlias thrived, while double hollyhocks and sweet peas reached for the sky. Hydrangea hung heavy with blooms, and *Nepeta* and lavender billowed from pots, mingling with the delicate petals of chocolate cosmos. If all this sounds just a little too idyllic, don't worry . . . we also got chickens.

Somewhere along the line, no doubt through the influence of images on social media, I had the crazy idea we should add chickens to the mix. It seemed the perfect way to round out our new-found "self-sufficiency" and would allow me to cross one more item off my grocery list (eggs of course, not chicken). I was confident that Paul wouldn't support this plan when I proposed it. You could have knocked me over with one of their feathers when he said, "That's what I was thinking!" Anyone in the know, as clearly we were not, would tell you that combining chickens and gardens is a terrible idea. Chickens, however, would strongly disagree with this view because chickens love gardens. Chickens love eating gardens. Chickens love scratching and bathing in gardens. If lawnmowers had feathers and constantly pooped, they would be chickens. My feet-first approach to life meant we had to learn all of this the hard way. There was many a moment I found myself craving roast chicken for dinner, but somehow the prospect of finding that first egg in the coop made all their annoying personal habits a little more bearable. Taller fences and more chicken wire also helped.

It's hard to put into words the harmony and calm our little garden created during such a difficult time. Perhaps it is best described as being like the comfort an extra quilt provides on a chilly night; not so much about the warmth but rather the sense of security offered from the added weight. It envelops you and makes you feel safe and protected, just as the side garden does when I find myself puttering about, lost in thought. I am only steps from the house and the realities of everyday life, but somehow among the flowers and vegetables, clipping and weeding with chickens foraging at my feet (their constant clucking a weirdly soothing soundtrack), I feel worlds away.

If I were to make a list of simple pleasures, socks that don't shriggle down when I walk would rank high, as would finding the cold side of my pillow in the night, or that little rush I get every time I connect another piece of whatever puzzle I'm working on. But time in the garden has shown me many more pleasures, and suddenly upright socks and cool pillows can't hold a candle to a freshly picked bowl of cherry tomatoes, still warm from the sun. Or the meditative quality of shelling fresh peas, or the pride that comes from sharing a bumper crop of zucchini with friends. A constant supply of fresh eggs and the scent of old-fashioned roses on my bedside table add a richness to everyday life that for me is without compare.

How do you ultimately decide what to grow in your garden? There are endless choices when it comes to vegetables, flowers, and herbs, not to mention the range of varieties to choose from within each selection. Do you grow a French radish or a watermelon radish? Butterhead, romaine, or loose-leaf lettuce? Black Tuscan or curly kale? And don't even get me started on all the tomato options out there.

I believe the simplest way to make your decision is to start by planting what you love to eat. If you fill a garden just as I did, with all your favorites, you'll be inspired every day to cook with the bounty you've grown and create new and delicious ways to enjoy them. One glance at my garden and the following pages will reveal my deep love for sweet English peas, tender greens, juicy tomatoes, crunchy cucumbers, zucchini, radishes, and wee alpine strawberries. Spending time in the garden every morning generally dictates what I'll be cooking for dinner that night for fresh produce is just that, and it's best consumed at its peak. The recipes in this book are a direct reflection of that very philosophy.

I don't consider myself an authority on pretty much anything (though I do now know an awful lot about chickens). I am always more passionate than I am professional, and I continually make mistakes. But I'm curious and a hard worker, traits that will ultimately help provide the continued education I'm seeking. I can't tell you everything you need to know about growing a garden, only what worked and what didn't for me. What I can tell you with total confidence and conviction, though, is that no matter how big your yard, your patio, or your balcony, whether you commit to a variety of vegetables or a single window box of herbs, I believe that tending to even the smallest piece of dirt will invariably bring you the greatest peace of mind.

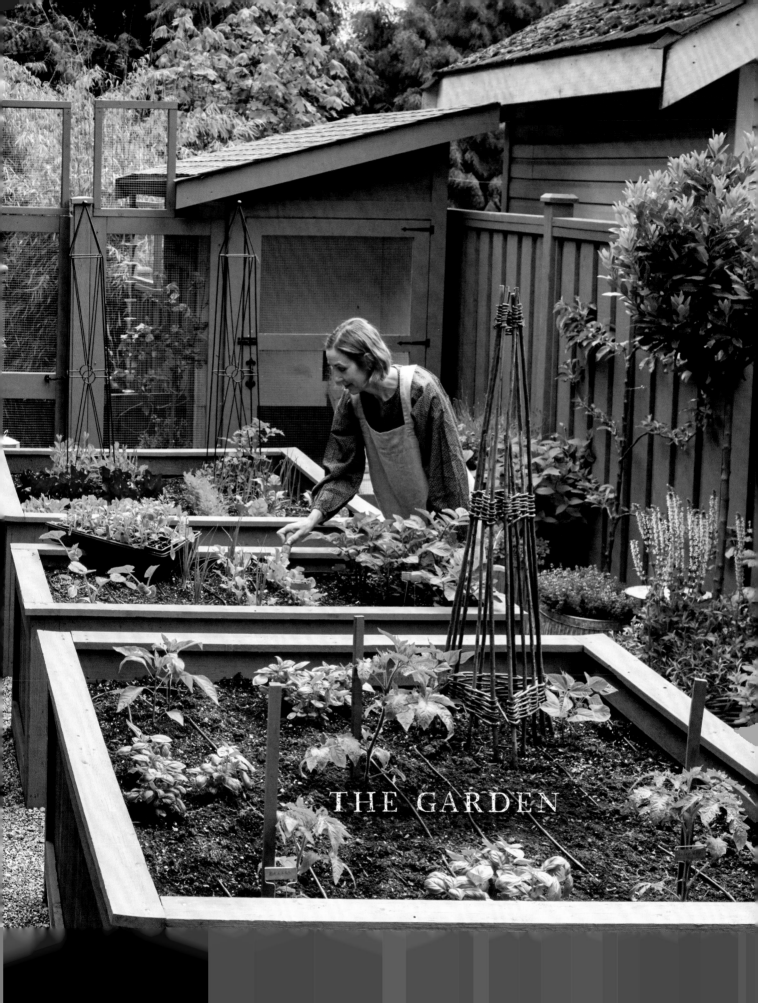

THE GARDEN

THE GARDEN

1. HYDRANGEAS

2. BOXWOOD HEDGES

3. TOMATOES AND BASIL

4. ZUCCHINI AND POTATOES

5. LETTUCE, KALE, CARROTS, AND PEAS

6. HERBS, CUCUMBERS, AND ROSES

7. POTTING BENCH

8. TOOL SHED

9. LADDERS

10. CHICKEN COOP

11. HEN'S DUST BATH

12. FOUNTAIN

13. CHICKEN RUN

14. WATER FEATURE

15. GREENHOUSE

16. SHED

A GOOD FOUNDATION

It's important to remember this isn't really a gardening book, but rather a book about my garden. I can't guide you on all the various styles of gardens and plant material available out there. I can only share with you the little I know and all that I love. I still rely heavily on books, Google, and the patience of my knowledgeable friends to help me on my own journey, and I encourage you to do the same. Never be afraid to ask lots of questions and make mistakes; it's the basis for a good education. Hopefully, should you be interested in or attracted to the images and advice on these pages, you'll find this book offers the inspiration and encouragement you need to get started on a garden of your very own.

When you think of gardening, what's the first thing that comes to mind? I'm guessing plants and soil. Naturally, when we envision a garden it's all about the plant material. But long before you can start digging holes and sprinkling seeds, you will want to give thoughtful consideration to the overall structure and design of the space, as ultimately every detail will play an integral part in the success of your garden.

I like to think there are no rules when designing a garden, other than to create a space that both you and your plants will enjoy. Ultimately what you're able to successfully grow will be limited by the exposure and square footage you have (a giant palm tree on a north-facing balcony probably isn't your best bet, and yet under those same conditions many other plants would thrive). But layout, materials, and theme play

an enormous role in determining the overall beauty and flow of your finished garden.

Many years ago, I began my career in interior design. I knew the importance of creating spaces that truly reflected my client's personality so that they always looked and felt at ease in their surroundings. This meant taking time to listen and observe so I could fully understand their interests and patterns. And so too, it goes with gardens. You want to give your plants and vegetables a home that speaks to their own style and nature as well as your own.

I have always loved more romantic flowers, much like you'd find in an English cottage garden. I like beds and planters that are densely planted, jammed full of climbing roses, viola, cosmos, and foxglove. There is a charm and informality they create that makes me incredibly happy while also providing the perfect framework for my vegetable beds. Unfortunately, a mature garden doesn't happen overnight. It can take perennial plants up to two years to fully develop a strong root system. When you see a beautiful garden wall covered in climbing roses, know that it was years in the making. With that in mind, you can start to see how important the look of the actual wall is while it waits for the rose to take over.

When designing the side garden, I wanted to first create a space that could visually hold its own until the plants and vegetables eventually took center stage. To achieve this, I gave a lot of thought to the materials and structure of the garden, always keeping in mind the desired style and theme I was envisioning. My goal

wasn't so much to grow award-winning tomatoes and roses, but rather to be transported through my humble efforts. I wanted a space to remind me of the many gardens Paul and I had visited on our travels through the English countryside. A space that was warm and inviting without feeling shiny and new, much as if you were stepping into a fond memory.

The following elements played a huge part in helping to make my side garden dream a reality, providing a backdrop that was both beautiful and functional.

FENCING: The first step in the transformation of the side garden was a proper fence. The old one was rotting and falling apart, and no amount of paint could disguise that. For me, the new fence immediately defined the space, and the interior layout followed. I chose cedar and finished it with an opaque stain by Benjamin Moore in Amherst Gray. I used this same stain on all the planter boxes, lattice work, and chicken coop for a cohesive and uniform look. I even stained a pile of stakes my handyman cut for me—an easy DIY for those with a great appreciation for detail. The gray is a perfect foil to the dark soil, various greens, and pastel shades of the plants and flowers.

LAYOUT: I needed to maximize the space we had for plantings but still be able to move easily about. Paul would argue that I've made it nearly impossible to get around the garden with the endless assortment of pots and baskets I've filled it with, but he's confused. I'm confident I can even squeeze in a few more. Our space ultimately allowed for four raised planters of varying sizes for vegetables and herbs, a new bed at the west end of the yard for cutting flowers and strawberries, and the chicken coop at the east end. With the garden being south facing, this layout ensured the vegetable beds and planters would receive lots and lots of sunshine. In addition to the raised planters, I also made sure to include a work bench for planting and a storage cabinet for all the unattractive but necessary bits and bobs you require to maintain your garden. I for one don't want to be distracted from the surrounding beauty by a bunch of plastic fertilizer containers.

LATTICE WORK: To further enhance the effect of the lush garden I desired, I looked to the walls with an "If you build it, they will come" attitude. My clematis and roses were very grateful that I had the forethought to provide for their needs and thanked me by quickly taking hold. Considering these sorts of details can save you a lot of time and effort further down the road, so do pay attention to how both you and the plants will use the garden. Any work done after the plants have established themselves, while not impossible, will be more challenging and you run the risk of damaging them. Take time to think it through so you only have to get that can of stain and paint brush out once!

PEA GRAVEL: One of my favorite design details in the side garden was our decision to use pea gravel under foot. On top of the overall look, which I love, it has many practical attributes. It is inexpensive and easy to install, though a strong back and some willing helpers will make it even easier. Pea gravel improves drainage, prevents weeds, and is incredibly satisfying to rake, like having your very own Zen garden. It is also a wonderful ground for the chickens to run around on given how easy it is to maintain by simply hosing away any messes they make. But of all the reasons to have pea gravel in your garden, for me, that lovely, satisfying crunchy sound it makes when you walk on it is number one.

STONE WALLS AND PATHWAYS: Introducing even a small amount of natural stone to the garden is another effective way of adding structural substance and texture. Creating a wall, building some steps or adding a simple edging are all good ways to use this natural material. The bed for cut flowers and strawberries at the west end of the garden came to be as a solution to a rather large problem: originally there was a large tree in that corner of the yard.

Long before we bought the house, a very aggressive ivy plant took up residence in that tree. Year over year the ivy consumed more and more of the tree, eventually resulting in its death (it's always a good idea to cut ivy off at the base should it set its sights on one of your trees, thereby stopping it in its tracks). We had the tree cut down long before the side garden was a reality, which left a large stump to contend with when we started to plan. Given the stump's proximity to the property line, it was nearly impossible to have it ground out, so I had to get creative. I decided the best plan of attack, like for all dirty secrets, would be to bury it. Paul and our dear friend Cam Murphy spent an afternoon building a dry stack basalt retaining wall. Once it was finished, we backfilled the bed with fresh soil, covering the stump in the process. We then positioned a large stone planter, filled with hydrangeas, atop the buried stump. And no one was any the wiser. I guess this was a rather long-winded way to tell you all about my little stone wall that made a huge difference in my garden and solved all my problems.

TREE REMOVAL AND GENERAL PRUNING: It's a good idea to consider any major pruning or tree removal that might be necessary when planning your garden. In our case, the east end of the yard had a huge, completely dead tree straddling the property line that blocked a lot of the morning sun. I reached out to our neighbor, and we agreed to split the cost of the removal. Tackling this project before planting the garden made the whole process much easier without the added fear of damaging anything. Sometimes issues of this scale can seem a little daunting, but later, when your plants are basking in that extra sunshine, you'll be glad you took it on.

POTS, PLANTERS, AND DOLLY TUBS: An integral part of creating a cohesive look and feel to your space is deciding on the shape and colors of the various vessels you'll be using around the garden. While I don't mind a mix of styles, I do think it's important to limit the variety to no more than three, so things don't get too chaotic looking. For the side garden I focused on rattan baskets, vintage metal dolly tubs, and some pale, aged terra-cotta. I have a rule that if I see a nice pot or planter that works within my scheme, and it's a good price, I grab it. Even if I don't have something to fill it with right away, given how challenging it can be to find nice, affordable containers, I know it will be a good investment further down the road (and a wonderful excuse to buy another plant . . . I hope Paul isn't reading this). I also splurged on a couple of antique planters that I felt really added to the atmosphere in the side garden; their lovely patina adds a weight and history that just can't be replicated with new pieces. Keep your eyes open at garage sales or second-hand stores for old pots or birdbaths should you want to achieve the same effect.

WATER FEATURE: I think the sound of running water in a garden should be mandatory, as a garden should appeal to all our senses. There is something so incredibly soothing about the burble of running water, helping to drown out the sounds of a city and letting you focus on the garden around you. I've discovered that a water feature or small fountain can be made for very little money. And they don't need to be elaborate to be effective. A large, glazed planter works beautifully. Simply use waterproof putty to seal the drainage hole in the bottom. Once placed in the garden and then filled with water, you can add a small basic pump if you have access to power or buy a solar-powered fountain to float about the surface. The bonus of the fountain is that the continual movement of the water will help prevent mosquitos hanging around and laying eggs on the surface of the water. If neither option is doable, a planter filled with still water and some floating plants is still lovely—just be sure to change the water regularly to avoid the aforementioned mosquito issue.

SEATING: If space allows, make sure to include a small bench or a couple of old bistro chairs and a table in the garden. As satisfying as it is to work in the garden, it's equally enjoyable to sit quietly among all the beauty you have created and enjoy a glass of wine. I had a beautiful concrete bench in the back of the garden that I loved to sit on when I visited with the

chickens. Unfortunately, my chickens soon discovered this same bench was the perfect launching pad they needed to help get them over the fence and into my vegetable planters. You just can't trust a chicken.

ACCESSORIES: Much like my (limited variety of) pots and planters, I give a lot of thought to the tools and accessories I use throughout the garden. It may seem a little "type A" to worry about the color of your garden hose, but for me those details matter. Why would I spend all this time and effort to create a beautiful and harmonious garden and then drag a neon-blue hose through it? My eyes! My eyes! All jokes aside, I do take great pleasure in choosing every item in the garden, from a watering can or rake right down to the brass plant tags that mark my beds. Just like the inside of my home, I feel every detail plays an integral part in the overall vision and harmony of the space.

GARDEN ESSENTIALS

It is one thing to have a beautiful garden structurally, but it also must function practically for your plants to truly be happy and thriving. Below you'll find a list of various elements and tips that will help to ensure their success.

SOIL: The first question any experienced gardener will ask when they hear you want to start a garden is, "Do you have good soil?" Because you see, I have learned that there is dirt and then there is *dirt*—and the health and vitality of your plants are dependent on the overall quality of your soil. Dark, rich soil, heavy in nutrients is the goal, and the soil you start with may require the addition of plenty of organic matter, otherwise known as compost, to get there. Adding compost to your existing soil will go a long way in improving its condition and ultimately the health of everything you are growing.

You can achieve this by purchasing bags of ready-made compost mixture and manure and working them into your beds or, if space allows, carving aside somewhere in the back of your yard for a pile or bin to do your own composting. Compost can be composed of a variety of ingredients, including grass clippings, leaves, and your daily kitchen scraps. If you're using a compost bin, I'd personally always choose an enclosed one to help keep rodents at bay. Mice and rats love nothing more than partying in a pile of food scraps.

In addition to organic matter, another way to improve your soil would be through aeration. Soil that has been packed down over the years tends not to hold water very well and is challenging to dig in. Spend some time using a pitchfork to lift and loosen your soil.

STAY IN YOUR ZONE: All plants require a specific set of conditions to thrive, with climate being one of the biggest factors. You'll notice on pretty much all plant tags at the nursery there will be a line describing plant hardiness with a corresponding range of numbers. These numbers represent climatic temperature zones and indicate where that plant will successfully grow. The map is created based on the average annual extreme minimum temperatures in zones across the country. The higher the number, the warmer the zone, with the lower numbers, one through three, indicating zones that regularly experience temperatures below freezing. It's important to take note of these details so that you aren't heartbroken by the loss of a beloved plant or tree that didn't make it through a chilly winter.

STARTS VERSUS SEEDS: Then comes the question of whether to grow your plants from seed or from starts. With starts, the name pretty much says it all. Instead of planting seeds inside first and transferring them outside when they're ready, you can simply buy small commercially ready-grown plants at your local nursery, thereby giving you and your garden a little head "start." Growing things from seeds can be very satisfying but it takes some planning and equipment (and if you don't have a greenhouse to work in, you'll soon find your living room looks like one). Having said that, many vegetables can be direct sown as soon as the weather permits.

This means you place the seeds directly into the garden bed as soon as the fear of any frost is gone (rather than having to start them inside first). Carrots, beans, radishes, and peas are some examples of vegetables you would direct sow, providing you almost instant results as their seeds germinate very quickly.

PLANT WHAT YOU CAN EAT: The seeds versus starts question leads me to a very important tip when planting a vegetable garden. Remember to plant not much more than you can actually consume. A little more is OK because then you'll have enough to share with your family and neighbors, but more than that and you'll find yourself sitting on a pile of produce. Tiny seeds and young plants can be deceptive. It might seem logical to sprinkle the entire package or plant that whole flat of young zucchini sprouts, but proceed with caution. Just like our stomachs at a buffet table, our eyes are always bigger than our garden beds! I learned this lesson when starting tomatoes from seed for the first time. I got a little greedy when shopping online, tempted by all the amazing and unique varieties on offer. Unable to settle on just one, I chose nine different kinds of tomato. Each little bag that arrived contained ten to fifteen seeds, and I happily planted them all! I quickly discovered how easily a tomato seed germinates. Within a matter of weeks, I was surrounded by more than 100 tomato plants! Anyone who visited my home was forced to leave with a plant or two, much to the confusion of the UPS delivery driver and meter reader.

IRRIGATION: I probably wouldn't even be writing this book if we hadn't installed a drip irrigation system in the side garden. That's because there would be no garden to write about. It would have died within a month of planting, leaving me to share only the depressing story of my abysmal failure. The truth of the matter is an irrigation system makes the garden a happier place. The plants are happy because they aren't dying of thirst, and I'm happy because Paul and I aren't squabbling over who will water the garden.

We chose a surface-mounted drip system that worked off our existing hose bib, which saved us a lot of money and works like a charm. I was hesitant at first, as

I fretted that the drip lines would look messy in the beds, but as the patient installer repeatedly assured me, they camouflaged nicely with the dirt. The plants are now watered every morning at 6:15 a.m. for about three minutes and that's it for the day! From an environmental standpoint, this seems very efficient. By keeping the beds lightly but consistently moist we aren't over-watering and wasting precious water in the height of summer. So to save your sanity, your relationship, and maybe even the planet, I encourage you to consider a drip irrigation system of some sort, especially if your garden faces south.

FERTILIZERS: In addition to improving your soil with compost and manure, your plants may require extra nutrients in the form of a liquid or granular fertilizer throughout the season to really flourish. This was a tip one of my brilliant gardener friends shared with me and it made a world of difference to the growth and health of my plants. Just as some people under-salt their cooking, I was under-fertilizing my flowerpots!

It's important to remember though that all plants have slightly different nutritional needs, so make sure to do your homework depending on the assortment you've chosen and follow the package instructions for use. I use organic fertilizers over synthetic whenever possible. Chemical fertilizers are made up of varying ratios of synthetic nitrogen, phosphorus, and potassium; they are made to feed your plants through a quick burst of nutrients that can sometimes be challenging for the plant to fully absorb, causing some of the fertilizer to run off during watering and ultimately make its way into the area's groundwater. Organic fertilizers, on the other hand, derive nutrients from natural sources like manure and compost, which also improves the soil texture, allowing it to hold water longer. This means the nutrients are less likely to run off into the groundwater. A side bonus is that manure and compost are full of life, containing zillions of microbes. Those living organisms go a long way toward improving the overall health of your soil, making it easier to work in and grow healthy plants without any fear of harming the planet.

Tools of the Trade

Having the right tools or instruments, no matter what the task, makes everything so much easier.

Just like my favorite wooden spoon or paring knife in the kitchen, these are the garden tools I am most attached to and reach for time and time again. Invest in the best you can afford, maintain them well, and they'll be working alongside you in the garden for a lifetime.

SECATEURS (PRUNING SHEARS): The hardest-working tool out there. I can't stress enough the importance and resulting satisfaction of owning a good, sharp pair of clippers. Maintain and sharpen them regularly with a cleaning stone, sharpening block, and a little tutorial on YouTube.

My shears are made by Okatsune in Japan, and I love them! They are a good weight and have a great locking mechanism with a nice sharp blade.

GLOVES: If I'm honest, I have amassed a pretty good collection of gardening gloves. Somehow, I always return from a trip to the nursery with another pair, but really, one good, washable pair and maybe a longer set for protection when pruning prickly roses or shrubs would suffice.

HAND TROWEL: A short-handled little workhorse. There is a lot of hole digging, transplanting, and weed removal in gardening and this is the tool that helps get it all done. They aren't all created equal, so make sure to test them out before you buy. You want one that sits comfortably in your hand with a good weight.

WEEDING HOE: Much like a regular hoe but with an open head, this tool makes weeding the garden a breeze. I like to have a short-handled one for the raised garden beds and one with a long handle for the flower beds so that I don't have to bend over while working.

RAKE: A standard metal leaf rake is a necessary tool in the side garden to help keep the pea gravel free of fallen leaves and debris. A smaller hand rake or cultivator is really handy for cleaning up the raised planters or turning soil while navigating around the plants and vegetables.

GARDEN HOSE WITH SPRAY NOZZLE: If you own chickens, then you already know how important a good garden hose is. My attached spray nozzle is permanently set to "jet" so that I can blast away at the pea gravel every night, cleaning up any surprises the chickens may have deposited earlier in the day. Sadly, I'm still on the hunt for my forever spray nozzle. I have yet to find one I can't break by the summer's end. If you are the manufacturer of a quality spray nozzle that doesn't leak, please call me. We need to talk.

GARDEN TWINE: Not just a pretty prop, twine is something I use plenty of throughout the summer. Whether I'm securing my tomatoes to stakes, my climbing roses to the trellis, or sweet peas to a metal obelisk, twine is the solution. I keep a big ball of it on the work bench with a pair of sharp scissors nearby.

STAKES: I am convinced I will never have enough garden stakes! I really underestimated their importance when I first started gardening, assuming I would only be needing them for the tomatoes. I soon discovered that dahlias topple over without them and one heavy rain will flatten all the cosmos if they don't have that extra support to save them. Bamboo stakes are great for smaller, finer plants, and 1-inch-by-1-inch cedar, in varying lengths, will do for all the others.

PLANT LABELS AND A MARKER: It is always a good idea to label your seedlings when planting (and even more so if you're direct sowing with seeds) so you don't forget what is growing where. In addition to the name of the flower or vegetable or its specific variety, I like to add the date it was planted. This is a good way to track a plant's progress or lack thereof.

WATERING CAN: The last time Paul and I visited England, I insisted on buying not one, but two watering cans. Thereby demonstrating what a strong marriage I have. In my defense, finding one attractive watering can is challenge enough, but two? Two is clearly a sign from the universe and must be seized upon immediately, regardless of where you are in the world or how small your suitcase.

SMALL WHEELBARROW: Consider this your garden's handbag, perfect for toting all its essentials around the yard. I like to keep it on the small side so it's easier to lift and maneuver.

TOOL BELT: This is a gardener's holster, so you can be the quickest draw with your clippers! A tool belt also keeps you from leaving your valuable tools somewhere in the garden bed. Pay attention when purchasing, as good tool belts come made for right- or left-handed gardeners.

GARDENING CLOGS: I'm happiest in my clogs. If I'm wearing them, it means I am in the garden. My clogs are made by Hunter, a company famous for rubber boots (or wellies, as the English call them), and I love them. Waterproof, easy to clean, and roomy enough to accommodate the sexy added layer of some woolly socks in the colder months. Am I the picture of style and sophistication wearing them? No. But I am bloody comfortable.

A WIDE-BRIMMED HAT (AND SUNSCREEN): It can get pretty warm in the garden at the height of summer, so I always make sure to pop on a hat with a nice wide brim and slather on lots of sunscreen, because no one wants heatstroke or a nasty burn. I love that my straw garden hat has a string that allows it to hang on my back when I don't need it but makes it easily accessible when I do.

AIR PODS: Music or an interesting podcast can be excellent company when weeding the garden.

It's Not All Sunshine and Roses

While some people fantasize about winning the lottery, my daydreams are all about bug- and blight-free gardens. It takes vigilance and a sharp eye to keep your flowers and vegetables healthy and free of disease. Every morning and evening I walk the garden and inspect for nibbles on leaves or mildew spots on the plants. It's important to lift the leaves, look at stems, and really give them a good once-over. Wilted leaves, black spots, or yellowing are all indicators that you might have a problem. Late in the evening, with your flashlight in hand, is also an ideal time to catch pests in the act when they come out to snack. The variety of bugs and ailments that can infest your garden is unfortunately long. Below are the most common issues I have personally encountered and some suggestions on how I chose to tackle them.

APHIDS: An annoying wee green sap-sucking insect that loves to hang out on the tender new shoots of a variety of plants. One effective way to rid your garden of aphids is to introduce them to ladybugs. Their new relationship won't last long, as ladybugs love to eat aphids. Your best weapon is your garden hose. Just give the infested plant a good hosing, blasting the aphids to oblivion. Aphids are wingless and usually lack the energy to make it all the way back to the plant. A spray of insecticidal soap or neem oil can also be helpful.

CUTWORMS: They come by their name honestly. Cutworms are most fond of young vegetable and fruit seedlings and enjoy chewing right through stems at ground level. If you notice your young plants suddenly toppling over, they've no doubt been the victim of a cutworm. You can avoid this by waiting to plant out your seedlings until they are a little bigger and better equipped to fend off attacks, or you can place collars around the base of your plants to protect them. Cutworm collars are commercially available, or you can make your own by cutting down plastic drinking cups.

MILDEW: Powdery mildew is a common fungus that can affect lots of plants but seems to particularly love my zucchini and tomato plants. It is caused by poor air circulation, the result of plants being too crowded or too close to a wall, and a lack of sunlight. The first step is always going to be about prevention. Space your plants to increase air flow and reduce humidity. Always work with clean tools, and remove and dispose of any affected leaves or stems in the garbage, rather than the compost to avoid future contamination. You can buy fungicidal sprays to battle mildew or create your own by mixing and filling a spray bottle with 1 tablespoon baking soda and ½ teaspoon liquid soap to 1 gallon (4 liters) of water. Make sure to spray all areas of the plant, including both sides of the leaves, liberally with the solution.

SLUGS: On top of being hideous little slimeballs, slugs also have a big appetite for most plants. They hide out somewhere shady during the day and emerge at night to feast. They are especially active during damp weather. It's best to hunt them down and handpick the slugs off your plants in the evening when they come out to dine. You can set out store-bought traps or make your own by burying an open jar or yogurt tub until it is level with the ground. Fill it halfway with any kind of beer, slugs aren't picky. As soon as they get a whiff they'll head right over, topple in, and drown.

YELLOWING LEAVES: Just as you should be careful to not forget to water your garden, it's equally important not to overwater it. Yellow leaves can be an indication of too much water or poor drainage, leaving your beds too wet. In overly wet soil, roots can't breathe, causing them to suffocate and stop doing their all-important job of delivering water and nutrients to your plants. Ironically, a lack of water has the same effect. So clearly, it's about finding the right balance. For very little money, you can buy a soil water meter, which will instantly let you know if you're watering your garden too much or too little.

VEGETABLE THOUGHTS

Below is a list of fruits and vegetables that I have had success with in my garden. Every year I look forward to growing all my favorites, but I also make a point to try one or two new items or varieties to keep things interesting, and I encourage you to do the same. It can be both fascinating and educational to discover how even the most basic vegetables reveal themselves in the garden as they grow.

ARUGULA, SPINACH, AND SALAD GREENS: There is nothing quite as lovely as a salad made from young, fresh leaves. You'll never look at lettuce at the supermarket the same way again, what with it being virtually tasteless by comparison. You can sow the seeds directly in the spring, but I prefer to start them earlier in the greenhouse or purchase small plants from the nursery to give them a head start. Tiny young leaves are very enticing to slugs and snails and really don't stand a chance against them. I have been told that a sprinkle of organic slug pellets or a border of copper tape is a good way to deter the slimy little menaces, but I believe the only sure way to remove them is two fingers and a flashlight after dark. It's a bit of work, but when I discover serious nibbles out of my plants, with a little dedication I can generally find the culprits (at which point I pitch them over the fence—I don't feel bad about this given my neighbors are a bunch of young guys who seem to grow more than their fair share of marijuana. I'm sure the slugs have way more fun in their yard).

BEETS: Beets like to grow in cooler temperatures. They enjoy the heat of the day but prefer a cooler evening.

This allows you to sow the seeds in the spring for a summer harvest, and then sow again later in summer for another round, harvesting the winter crop after the first hard frost. Just as delicious as the root vegetable itself, the leafy green tops of beets are an excellent alternative to kale or Swiss chard, so consider them a twofer!

BROCCOLI: Broccoli is one of those vegetables that comes as a real surprise when it starts to take shape. From deep in the center of its big green leaves, one day a little broccoli head emerges!

Just like beets and kale, broccoli is a cool-season crop, meaning you'll need to plant it in early spring or late summer to make sure that you are harvesting it before or after the high heat of summer. Once you harvest the main head, hang in there, as the broccoli will continue to produce smaller heads from side shoots for weeks to come.

CARROTS: Carrots are a vegetable best sown direct (meaning you'll plant the seeds exactly where you plan to grow them) as they don't like to be transplanted and have their roots disturbed. Sprinkle the seeds lightly, trying to leave a little space between each one to allow for initial growth. Once the carrots get going, you will no doubt need to thin them again but do not worry about waste; carrots are delicious no matter how small, so you can eat the wee ones you had to sacrifice for sake of the larger ones still to come. In lieu of your standard orange carrot, I like to grow a rainbow blend, producing carrots in shades of purple, red, white, and yellow, which makes for a beautiful presentation when entertaining.

CUCUMBERS: A very easy vegetable to grow if provided with plenty of sun, water, and a spot to climb. They also love very fertile soil, so make sure to amend your soil with a rich compost before planting to give them the best start. Like zucchini, the speed at which a cucumber grows is rather mind boggling. The tiniest of cucumbers at dusk are somehow fully grown by breakfast.

I know this because my husband, Paul, likes to leave me gifts of random produce he has collected when returning from letting the chickens out.

I have discovered many a cucumber next to my cereal bowl when I sit down in the morning.

ENGLISH PEAS: I adore English peas (also known as shelling peas) and not just because they are delicious!

I would grow them even if I hated the taste, as I love the beauty and height they bring to the garden. With their squiggly little tendrils and pods plump with peas, they hang from their vines like little Christmas tree ornaments, and I can't help but smile. They are simple to grow in full sun or partial shade with consistent watering, but supports are a must. You can use either netting on a wall or a trellis teepee made of branches to offer the tender vines something to grasp when climbing. English peas are quick to mature, generally ready for picking fifty-five to eighty days from the time seeds are sown, and while the shells themselves aren't edible, all other parts of the plant are—including the shoots and tendrils, which are lovely tucked in salads and sandwiches.

FENNEL: Not everyone is a fan of fennel's distinctive licorice taste, but I'm not one of those people. I love fennel.

I love it shaved in salads and sandwiches, roasted, grilled, or even juiced! I also love to use the fluffy tops, chopped or torn, as a delicious garnish for greens or fish dishes.

On top of all that, fennel is also a gorgeous ornamental plant, so you have no excuse not to try it! It will need at least six hours of sun a day and an evenly moist soil, so avoid overwatering.

HERBS: If you only grow one thing, choose herbs. Without a doubt, I think they offer the greatest bang for your effort and buck given how much they can improve the flavor of what we eat and drink. You might not have the space to raise chickens, but simply adding a handful of fresh herbs to store-bought eggs will make your next omelet infinitely better, as does adding them to salad dressing, marinades, and grilled fish and meat, steeping them for tea, or even adding them to ice cubes. Herbs are easy and inexpensive to grow and are happy in pots, making them ideal for even the smallest space—and when summer is over you can dry or freeze them to use all winter long. The choices are endless, but at a bare minimum I would grow parsley, rosemary, thyme, chives, dill, basil, and mint.

KALE: The best way to get those dark, leafy greens in your diet is to grow kale!

Kale is just as happy in your garden bed as it is in a pot, making it a great choice if your growing space is limited to a patio or deck. Kale is also a very hardy plant, allowing you to sow seeds in late summer to harvest throughout the winter, even under snowfall! No other vegetable tries this hard to get you to like it. My favorite variety would be cavolo nero, also known as Tuscan kale or black kale.

POTATOES: I LOVE growing potatoes. If I'm being honest, the growing isn't actually that exciting, but digging them up at the end of summer is a riot! It is like an edible treasure hunt—and once you've eaten a fresh boiled new potato with lots of butter and salt, you too will LOVE growing potatoes. They require full sun, and their green tops get quite big, so make sure you give them some space to grow. Having said that, you can also easily plant a couple of seed potatoes in a pot, and they'll still do their thing.

RADISHES: Growing radishes is good for your ego. Given how quickly and easily they mature, you'll be convinced that you're some sort of gardening savant. Just a little sprinkle on day one will yield wee shoots by the week's end, and before you know it, you'll be inviting neighbors over for drinks and crackers smothered in radish butter. Radishes have few demands other than full sun and water, but it is important not to overcrowd them or each radish won't have the space it needs to grow nice and full. If you find you have overseeded, simply thin things out by pulling up some of the new shoots as they start to grow to create more room. Some of my favorite varieties are Easter Egg and French Breakfast.

RHUBARB: Just like my reasoning for growing English peas, rhubarb is another wonderful plant that is as gorgeous to look at as it is delicious to eat. So much so that I chose to plant my rhubarb patch in one of the flower beds as I think its glossy big leaves and pink stalks are a lovely contrast mingling with the roses and lavender. That being said, I also can't wait to start picking and cooking with it come early spring. I love the tartness of rhubarb and think it works beautifully in a huge variety of baking, but it is equally delicious cooked down with sugar and spices to create the perfect condiment for burgers and sandwiches (Rhubarb Ketchup recipe on page 134) or a compote for topping oatmeal or yogurt. Just remember that rhubarb likes lots of sunshine and lightly moist soil; too much water and its roots will get soggy and rot.

STRAWBERRIES: Here is the difference between 99% of the strawberries you purchase in the grocery store and those from your garden or the farmers' market during the summer months: one tastes like a strawberry and the other tastes like wood. And strawberries are one of the easiest fruits to grow. They are happy in a pot or a patch and not too picky about their soil, as long as they get at least six hours of sun a day. When deciding on what strawberry to grow, make sure to select one of the "everbearing" varieties instead of those that are "June-bearing" so that you continue to get strawberries

throughout the whole of the summer season. The everbearing variety Seascape is one of my favorites because its berries are just as red on the inside as they are on the outside!

TOMATOES: The crown jewel of the vegetable garden. Of all the things one can grow, for some reason presenting a perfectly ripe, juicy tomato to most people will elicit the kinds of oohs and ahhs generally reserved for the Holy Grail.

Fortunately, tomato seeds are one of the easiest to germinate, which can feel incredibly rewarding for a new gardener. The real work is actually in finding a suitable location for your plants to grow, as tomatoes require a true hot spot to thrive. They need at least seven to eight hours of direct sun a day, so choose their home wisely. With too little sun, your plants will become leggy in their attempt to find the light. The fruit will also be smaller and take longer to ripen. There are soooo many tomato varieties out there, but two of my favorites are Amethyst Jewel and Black Beauty. I will always consider slices of homegrown tomato on toast with lots of mayo a perfect meal.

ZUCCHINI: One of the most versatile vegetables to grow because of the endless ways to cook it. You can roast it, grill it, pickle it, fry it, or eat it just as it comes. I am a big fan of it in all of its states, but I especially love raw zucchini noodles in place of traditional spaghetti. Zucchini plants can be started from seed indoors and transplanted once the fear of frost is gone or you can sow direct once the weather warms in late spring or early summer.

Zucchini is a thirsty, sun-loving plant with very large leaves that spreads quickly, so consider this when choosing a spot for it in your garden bed; in general zucchini will need 3 to 4 feet on either side of the plant for ideal growth. With regular watering and a weekly liquid fertilizer, each plant should yield about sixteen zucchini. I like to harvest my zucchini when they are only 5 to 6 inches in length, as younger squash is more tender and flavorful than its larger self.

THE RECIPES

SNACKS & APPETIZERS

CUCUMBER STICKS WITH CHILI FLAKES & SEA SALT

English cucumber(s), sliced

Sprinkle of chili flakes

Sprinkle of sea salt

This recipe, like Brown Butter (page 199), isn't so much a recipe as a method, and it makes one of my favorite little nibbles to put out when having friends over for drinks or if I'm in need of a quick mid-afternoon snack. You can just adjust the amounts based on the number of people to feed. If you've chosen to grow long English cucumbers, you'll want to slice them in half before quartering them, or you could also plant a patch of the baby English variety and skip that step. Either way, if the cucumber is particularly thick, you may want to halve your quarters to make thinner pieces.

Pile the sliced cucumbers on a serving plate and liberally sprinkle with chili flakes and sea salt. Ridiculously simple but ridiculously delicious!

MINTY PEAS ON TOAST WITH PECORINO & CHILI FLAKES

MAKES 4 TO 6 SERVINGS

This makes a fantastic appetizer for a group or a delicious lunch for you—just use a bigger slice of bread!

Toasts

1 nice chewy baguette

2 tablespoons olive oil

1 teaspoon salt

Minty Peas

1 tablespoon olive oil

1 shallot, finely diced

2 cups/280 g shelled fresh peas (frozen works too)

2 tablespoons finely chopped fresh parsley

2 tablespoons finely chopped fresh mint

1 tablespoon lemon juice

Zest of 1 lemon

⅓ cup/30 g finely grated pecorino cheese

½ teaspoon chili oil

1 teaspoon salt

Final Touches

Shaving of pecorino

Sprinkle of lemon zest

Sprinkle of finely chopped fresh mint

Sprinkle of chili flakes

Drizzle of olive oil

Move the oven rack to the top third of the oven. Preheat the broiler to high. Line a baking sheet with parchment paper.

TO MAKE THE TOASTS: Use a bread knife to slice twelve pieces of the baguette, each about ½ inch/1.25 cm thick. Use a pastry brush to lightly coat both sides of each piece with olive oil and then lay them face up on the baking sheet. Sprinkle with the salt and then place them under the broiler to broil for a minute or so, just until lightly toasted and starting to brown. Turn the bread over and repeat on the other side (no need to add more salt). Once done, remove the bread slices from the oven and set aside to cool.

TO MAKE THE MINTY PEAS: In a large frying pan over medium heat, warm the olive oil and sauté the diced shallot until soft and translucent, 3 to 4 minutes. Add the peas and continue to cook until they've just softened, another 3 to 4 minutes.

Transfer the peas and shallot to the bowl of a food processor. Add the parsley, mint, lemon juice, lemon zest, cheese, chili oil, and salt and blend until just combined but not smooth.

TO SERVE: Spread each piece of toast with the pea mixture and top with a shaving of pecorino, a sprinkle of lemon zest, chopped mint, some chili flakes, and a drizzle of olive oil.

RADISH BUTTER WITH NUTTY FRUIT CRACKERS

MAKES ABOUT 2 CUPS/
454 G BUTTER

2 cups/230 g fresh radishes,
   washed, dried, and finely
   grated (see Note)

1 cup/227 g "European style"
   unsalted butter (see Note)

1 tablespoon lemon juice

1½ teaspoons sea salt, plus
   more for sprinkling

Nutty Fruit Crackers
   (page 46), to serve

Radishes and butter are a match made in heaven but are usually served side by side, with a little bowl of sea salt for sprinkling. I decided to streamline the process by combining all the same elements into a delicious and fluffy radish butter. Made even more delicious when spread across a fruit cracker. Just keep sowing your radish seeds throughout the summer so you have a continuous supply.

Heap the grated radish in the middle of a double layer of cheesecloth. Twist the top closed and give the bundle a good squeeze to remove any excess liquid. Repeat this several times until the radish is very dry.

In a stand mixer fitted with the paddle attachment, whip the butter and lemon juice until light and fluffy. Add the grated radish and salt and mix to combine.

Place the radish butter in a large ramekin or small serving dish. Smooth over the top and sprinkle with a little more sea salt. The butter will keep in the refrigerator for several days, but do allow it to warm slightly before serving to make it easier for spreading on crackers.

NOTE: *When grating the radishes, I like to use my food processor to save time and my knuckles as grating small things can be a little risky. "European" butter has a higher fat content than standard butter and is creamier and richer in flavor. This recipe will work just fine with regular butter, but if you're using a salted butter just omit the sea salt.*

Continued

NUTTY FRUIT CRACKERS

MAKES ABOUT 36 CRACKERS

1 cup/120 g all-purpose flour

¼ cup/50 g firmly packed
   dark brown sugar

1 teaspoon baking powder

½ teaspoon salt

¼ cup/40 g raisins

¼ cup/40 g dried cherries

¼ cup/35 g roughly chopped
   hazelnuts

¼ cup/35 g roughly chopped
   pistachios

¼ cup/37.5 g roughly chopped
   dried apricots

¼ cup/47.5 g roughly chopped
   dried figs

1 tablespoon finely chopped
   fresh rosemary

½ cup/125 ml buttermilk

2 tablespoons butter, melted

Preheat the oven to 350°F/180°C. Butter an 8-inch/20 cm loaf pan and set aside.

In a large bowl, combine the flour, sugar, baking powder, and salt with the raisins, dried cherries, hazelnuts, pistachios, apricots, figs, and rosemary. Stir to combine. Add the buttermilk and stir to combine. The dough is quite dry, so I find it best to use my hands for the final mixing to make it all come together nicely.

Press the dough evenly into the prepared loaf pan. Bake for approximately 30 minutes or until a wooden skewer inserted into the center of the loaf comes out clean.

Remove the loaf from the oven and set aside until just cool enough to be removed from the pan. Allow the loaf to cool completely on a wire rack before cutting. I will often prepare the crackers to this point the night before and then cut and bake them again the next day. I find it much easier to slice the loaf thinly once it has sat for a bit.

Using a serrated knife, carefully slice each cracker very thinly and lay them on a parchment-lined baking sheet. Use a pastry brush to lightly coat the face-up side of each cracker with the melted butter.

Bake for 15 to 20 minutes, until a lovely golden brown.

You can store the cooled crackers in an airtight container for at least one week or in the freezer for 3 months.

WEE PEA PANCAKES WITH SMOKED SALMON

MAKES ABOUT EIGHTEEN
2-INCH/5 CM PANCAKES

Wee Pea Pancakes

2 handfuls fresh peas
  (or frozen)

1 cup/225 g full-fat cottage
  cheese

2 large eggs

2 tablespoons butter, melted

⅓ cup/40 g all-purpose flour

½ teaspoon baking powder

1 teaspoon salt

½ teaspoon pepper

1 teaspoon finely chopped
  fresh parsley

1 teaspoon finely chopped
  fresh dill

To Serve

½ cup/120 g crème fraîche

1 oz/28 g smoked salmon lox

Fresh dill, chopped, for garnish

Lemon zest, for garnish

Pepper, for garnish

Another wonderful excuse to grow English peas, this recipe makes a lovely appetizer for a crowd, a nice starter for a dinner party, or, with the addition of a little side salad, a perfect summer dinner for two. Simply adjust the size of the pancake to suit your needs.

TO MAKE THE PANCAKES: Place the peas in a small saucepan and fill with just enough water to cover them. Bring to a boil over high heat, lower the temperature to just a simmer, and cover. Simmer for 5 to 7 minutes, until they are just tender. If you're using frozen peas, 2 minutes should do the job. Drain the peas and set aside to cool.

Place the cottage cheese, cooled peas, eggs, and melted butter in a blender and blend on high until smooth. Add the flour, baking powder, salt, and pepper and blend again until mostly smooth. Add the parsley and dill and pulse a couple of times just to combine.

Place a nonstick pan over medium-high heat. Use a spoon or small scoop to drop portions of pancake batter into the hot pan, approximately 1 tablespoon per pancake. Flip the pancakes over when bubbles begin to rise to the surface and they are lightly browning on the bottom, about 2 minutes. Adjust the heat as necessary to keep them from burning. Cook the second side for about a minute more, just until browned. Transfer the pancakes to a cooling rack and repeat with the balance of the batter.

TO SERVE: Place the pancakes on a platter or serving tray and top with a teaspoon of crème fraîche and a little piece of smoked salmon. Garnish with a bit of dill, a sprinkle of lemon zest, and a quick grind of fresh pepper.

MARINATED ZUCCHINI WITH BURRATA

MAKES 4 SERVINGS

Marinated Zucchini

3 tablespoons olive oil

1 tablespoon white wine vinegar

2 tablespoons finely chopped basil

1 teaspoon chili flakes

1 teaspoon salt

½ teaspoon pepper

3 medium zucchini, cut into 2-inch/5 cm pieces

Dressing

1 tablespoon lemon juice

Zest of 1 lemon

¼ cup/60 ml olive oil

1 handful fresh mint leaves, finely chopped

1 tablespoon capers, roughly chopped

1 large ball fresh burrata cheese

Pinch of sea salt flakes

I first tried a dish like this while enjoying lunch at Petersham Nurseries in England, a beautiful garden center and café located near the river in Richmond. It truly is one of my most favorite spots on earth, providing endless inspiration everywhere you look. As much as I would love to pack up the whole place and take it home in my suitcase, I recognize the logistical challenges that would create. Instead, I am happy just trying to recreate a little of that beauty in my own kitchen and garden.

TO MAKE THE MARINATED ZUCCHINI: First make the marinade. In a large bowl, place 2 tablespoons of the olive oil, the vinegar, basil, chili flakes, salt, and pepper and whisk to combine.

In a large heavy-bottomed frying pan, heat the remaining 1 tablespoon of olive oil over medium-high heat. Place the zucchini in the pan in a single layer (if the pan is too small to accomplish this, you will have to work in batches to avoid crowding). Cook the zucchini until it starts to brown, using a spatula to turn the pieces as needed to brown all sides, 5 to 10 minutes. Once browned, transfer the zucchini to the large bowl and gently toss with the marinade.

TO MAKE THE DRESSING: In a small bowl, place the lemon juice and zest. Slowly add the olive oil while whisking until fully combined. Add the mint and capers and whisk again.

Use a large slotted spoon to transfer the marinated zucchini to a serving platter and top with the ball of burrata. Then spoon the dressing over the burrata and zucchini and sprinkle with a smidge of sea salt. When serving, simply scoop through the ball of burrata to break it up and enjoy!

VEGETABLE FRITTERS WITH CURRIED YOGURT

MAKES 4 TO 6 SERVINGS
(12 TO 18 FRITTERS)

Vegetable Fritters

1 teaspoon cumin seed, toasted
    and crushed

1 teaspoon coriander seed,
    toasted and crushed

2 cups/250 g grated zucchini

¾ cup/85 g self-rising flour

½ teaspoon salt

1½ cups/75 g grated carrot

1 tablespoon finely chopped
    chives

1 tablespoon finely chopped
    fresh dill

1 tablespoon finely chopped
    fresh mint

⅓ cup/80 ml buttermilk

1 large egg

Vegetable oil for frying

Curried Yogurt

1 cup/250 ml Greek-style plain
    yogurt

2 teaspoons curry powder

1 small handful fresh mint
    leaves, finely chopped

This batter is a great little vehicle for vegetables to get around in, so have some fun with it and experiment with the vegetables you use. I chose carrots and zucchini here, but depending on what your garden has to offer, fennel, corn, peppers, or finely grated cabbage would also be delicious alternatives or additions.

TO MAKE THE VEGETABLE FRITTERS: In a small frying pan over medium-high heat, toast the cumin and coriander seeds until they begin to brown and are fragrant. Transfer the seeds to a mortar and pestle to finely crush. If you don't own a mortar and pestle you could use the underside of a cast iron skillet atop a cutting board.

Place the grated zucchini in a piece of cheesecloth, twist it tightly, and give a good squeeze to remove as much liquid as possible.

In a large mixing bowl, combine the flour, salt, toasted seeds, grated carrot, zucchini, and chopped herbs. Stir to combine and evenly coat the vegetables.

In a small bowl, whisk together the buttermilk and egg. Add liquid to the vegetable mixture and stir to combine.

Place a large frying pan filled with 1 inch/2.5 cm of vegetable oil over medium-high heat until the oil reaches 370°F/190°C on a deep-fry thermometer. Very carefully drop heaping tablespoons of batter into the hot oil, making sure to be gentle to prevent any splashing.

Let the fritters cook until browned on the bottom, 2 to 3 minutes. Flip each fritter over using a spatula and repeat on the other side for 2 to 3 minutes more.

Carefully remove the fritters from the oil and transfer to a plate lined with paper towel to drain. Repeat with the balance of the batter (you can keep the fritters warm in a low oven, 225°F/105°C while finishing up).

TO MAKE THE CURRIED YOGURT: Place the yogurt, curry powder, and chopped mint in a small bowl and stir to combine.

Serve the fritters on a large platter alongside the yogurt dipping sauce. They are best served right away, but any leftovers will keep, covered, in the refrigerator for a day or two.

PICKLED CARROTS WITH DILL

MAKES 2 LARGE MASON
JARS

1½ cups/375 ml water

1½ cups/375 ml white vinegar

¼ cup/50 g sugar

1 tablespoon salt

2 stems fresh dill

2 teaspoons mustard seeds

2 teaspoons chili flakes

1 pound/454 g carrots, washed,
    peeled, and cut into
    ½-inch/1.25 cm thick sticks

Pickled vegetables are one of my favorite snacks to serve with drinks before dinner; a real step up from your average crudité platter. Like the recipe for Rhubarb Rosemary Shrub (page 61), the method here is straightforward, and the carrots and dill can be swapped out for a variety of other vegetables and herbs from your garden. The vinegar is a wonderful preserver, so the veggies will keep, covered, in the fridge for several weeks.

In a small pot over high heat, combine the water, vinegar, sugar, and salt. Bring the mixture to a boil and cook just until the sugar has dissolved. Remove from the heat.

Wash and dry two mason jars, about 1½ cups/375 ml each. Divide the dill, mustard seeds, and chili flakes between the two jars and then fill them with the carrot sticks. The carrots should fit snugly in the jars.

Using a funnel or large measuring jug, carefully fill each jar with the pickling liquid, making sure to fully cover the vegetables and herbs to about 1 inch/2.5 cm from the top. Screw the lids on the jars and place in the refrigerator for at least 48 hours before eating.

NOTE: *Other veggies that are delicious when pickled: green beans (quickly blanch them first in boiling water to bring out their color and then rinse in ice water); asparagus (like green beans, give a quick blanch to bring out their color); radishes; cucumbers; fennel.*

ROASTED CARROT DIP

MAKES A GENEROUS BOWL

Dip

1 pound/454 g carrots, peeled
  and cut into 1-inch/2.5 cm
  pieces (reserve some of the
  carrot greens for garnish)

1 tablespoon olive oil

1 tablespoon honey

1 teaspoon cumin

1 teaspoon cayenne

1 teaspoon salt

½ teaspoon pepper

2 cups/330 g chickpeas,
  drained and rinsed (reserve
  ¼ cup/40 g for garnish)

1 cup/140 g cashews, roasted
  and salted (if you use plain
  cashews add 1 teaspoon salt
  when blending)

1 cup/250 ml water

¼ cup/60 ml olive oil

¼ cup/60 ml lemon juice

To Serve

1 teaspoon lightly torn carrot
  greens

1 teaspoon lemon zest

Drizzle of olive oil

Sprinkle of sea salt

Spelt Herb Flatbread Crackers
  (page 59)

I can't imagine a more delicious way to use up a bounty of carrots while also improving your eyesight.

Serve alongside a basket of Spelt Herb Flatbread Crackers (page 59) for an appetizer or spread atop a thick slice of toast for lunch.

TO MAKE THE DIP: Preheat the oven to 400°F/200°C. Line a baking sheet with parchment paper.

Spread the carrots across the prepared baking sheet. Drizzle with the olive oil and honey, and sprinkle with the cumin, cayenne, salt, and pepper. Give the pan a little shake to roll the carrots around and coat them.

Bake for 25 to 30 minutes, giving the carrots a little stir at the halfway mark to ensure even browning, until fork tender.

On a separate baking sheet or small baking pan place the ¼ cup/43 g of reserved chickpeas. Sprinkle them with a little olive oil and salt. Roast for approximately 10 minutes, until golden brown and crunchy. Set aside.

In a food processor, combine the cashews, water, and remaining chickpeas and blend on high until smooth. Add the roasted carrots, olive oil, and lemon juice and blend again until mostly combined. I like the dip to still be a little chunky and have texture.

TO SERVE: Transfer the dip to a serving bowl. Top with the roasted chickpeas, carrot greens, lemon zest, a drizzle of olive oil, and a sprinkle of sea salt. Serve with spelt herb flatbread crackers.

The dip keeps, covered, in the fridge for up to 1 week.

SPELT HERB FLATBREAD CRACKERS

MAKES 4 GIANT CRACKERS
YOU'LL ENJOY BREAKING
INTO SMALLER ONES

1½ cups/180 g all-purpose flour

½ cup/55 g spelt flour

1 teaspoon baking powder

1 teaspoon salt

1 teaspoon finely chopped
    fresh rosemary

1 teaspoon fresh thyme leaves

¾ cup/180 ml water

¼ cup/60 ml olive oil

1 egg, beaten

1 teaspoon fresh thyme leaves

1 tablespoon finely grated
    parmesan (optional)

1 teaspoon sea salt

Preheat the oven to 400°F/200°C. Line two baking sheets with parchment paper.

In a large bowl, combine the all-purpose flour, spelt flour, baking powder, salt, rosemary, and thyme. Stir to combine.

Make a well in the middle of the dry ingredients and add the water and olive oil. Stir with a wooden spoon until mostly combined.

Turn the dough out onto the counter and knead several times until a smooth ball forms.

Divide the dough into four pieces. Using a rolling pin on a lightly floured surface, roll each piece of dough out until very thin, approximately ⅛ inch/ 3 mm thick. Each piece should be about 12 inches/30 cm long and 5 inches/12 cm wide.

Place two crackers side by side on each prepared baking sheet. Lightly brush with the beaten egg and sprinkle with the thyme leaves, parmesan (if using), and salt.

Bake for 10 to 12 minutes, until the crackers are slightly puffed and golden. Remove from the oven and allow to completely cool before snapping into smaller pieces.

These crackers will keep in an airtight container or bag easily for 1 week.

RHUBARB ROSEMARY SHRUB (WITH OPTIONS GALORE)

MAKES ABOUT 2 CUPS/500 ML
(ENOUGH FOR LOTS OF
DRINKS!)

2 cups/200 g washed, trimmed,
1-inch/2.5 cm pieces
rhubarb (see Note)

2 cups/400 g sugar

2 cups/500 ml apple cider
vinegar

2 to 3 rosemary stems,
6 inches/15 cm long

Tonic or carbonated water,
to serve

Somewhere between a medicinal cordial and a mocktail sits the shrub, a vintage mixer created using fruit, sugar, and vinegar. Paired with ice and tonic water, it proves to be one of my truly favorite drinks. The method is simple and leaves lots of room to play with different combinations, so let your imagination run wild and have some fun with it! If it's been a particularly long day, the addition of a little vodka or gin works well too.

In a large pot over medium-high heat, combine the rhubarb (or other fruit of your choice) and sugar. Cook for several minutes until the sugar has dissolved. Add the vinegar and rosemary and stir just to combine. Remove the pot from the heat.

Transfer the fruit mixture to a bowl or container with lid. Cover and let stand on the counter for at least 48 hours.

Line a sieve with cheesecloth and strain the shrub mixture into a large glass measuring cup. You can lift the cheesecloth by all four corners at the end and give it a little squeeze to extract any last juices.

Fill a large glass bottle with the shrub and store it in the fridge. The vinegar is the ultimate preserver, so it will keep for several months nicely.

To serve, fill a glass with some ice and 2 teaspoons of shrub mixture and top with tonic or carbonated water. Stir to combine and enjoy!

NOTE: *As promised, this recipe has options galore . . . Instead of rhubarb and rosemary, try raspberry and thyme, blackberry and mint, blueberry and lavender, or strawberry and basil.*

SALADS

ROASTED RED PEPPER & CANNELLINI BEAN SALAD

MAKES 4 SERVINGS

Roasted Red Pepper and Bean Salad

2 red peppers

3 handfuls baby arugula leaves, washed and dried

1 can (14 fl oz/398 ml/396 g) cannellini beans, drained and rinsed

⅓ cup/60 g mixed Sicilian pitted olives, roughly chopped

⅓ cup/40 g crumbled feta cheese

5 to 6 sundried tomatoes, roughly chopped

1 handful fresh basil leaves, roughly torn

⅓ cup/45 g pine nuts, lightly toasted

Dressing

1 tablespoon lemon juice

½ teaspoon pepper

¼ teaspoon salt

3 tablespoons olive oil

A simple salad that highlights three very easy things to grow: arugula, peppers, and basil. I guess if I lived in Italy I could add the olives to that list.

TO MAKE THE SALAD: Preheat the oven to broil on high. Line a baking sheet with foil. Place the oven rack near the center point of the oven, as you don't want the baking sheet too close to the broiler, which could char the peppers before they are actually roasted through.

Lay the peppers on their sides on the prepared baking sheet and place under the broiler. Use tongs to turn the peppers every 5 minutes or so until they are roasted and charred, about 15 minutes. Remove the peppers from the oven, place them in a paper bag, and fold the top to close it. Allow the peppers to steam for about 15 minutes.

Remove the peppers from the bag and use a small knife to scrape away the skin; now that they have steamed, their skins should come away very easily. Slice each pepper open, remove and discard the stem and the remaining seeds, and roughly chop. Transfer to a large serving bowl.

Add the arugula, beans, olives, feta, tomatoes, basil, and pine nuts to the bowl and use two spoons to toss to combine.

TO MAKE THE DRESSING: In a small bowl, whisk together the lemon juice, pepper, and salt. Slowly add the olive oil while continuing to whisk, until fully combined.

Dress the salad and toss again to serve.

SIDE GARDEN PANZANELLA SALAD

Salad

4 thick slices sourdough bread, cut into 1-inch/2.5 cm cubes

2 tablespoons olive oil

1 teaspoon flaky sea salt

1 teaspoon Italian seasoning

¼ pound/113 g green beans, trimmed

4 large tomatoes, seeds removed and cut into 8 wedges each

1 cup/140 g fresh English peas

6 to 8 radishes, thinly sliced

1 English cucumber, cut into 1-inch/2.5 cm pieces

1 big handful arugula

1 handful fresh basil leaves, roughly torn

2 tablespoons finely chopped fresh chives

Dressing

2 tablespoons white wine vinegar

2 teaspoons Dijon mustard

½ teaspoon salt

½ teaspoon pepper

½ cup/125 ml olive oil

Many of the recipes in this book allow for a lot of flexibility on the produce used, given that we might not all choose to grow the same things—so don't hesitate to switch things up in this salad if you need to. You can always replace the arugula with another leaf of your choice or green beans with asparagus. You could use raw beets in place of the radishes or chunks of zucchini in lieu of cucumber, but trust me when I tell you there is no substitute for the goodness of toasty, salty, olive oily bread chunks.

TO MAKE THE SALAD: Preheat the oven to 375°F/190°C and line a baking sheet with parchment paper.

Place the cubed bread pieces in a large bowl and drizzle with the olive oil. Use your hands or a large spoon to toss and coat the pieces.

Spread the bread across the prepared baking sheet and sprinkle with sea salt and Italian seasoning. Place in the preheated oven for 10 minutes, until the bread is just starting to get a little crispy and brown. Remove the bread from the oven and allow it to cool.

Bring a small pot of salted water to a boil over high heat. Gently lower the trimmed green beans into the boiling water and allow them to cook for 2 to 3 minutes, until a lovely bright green. Remove the beans from the heat and drain through a colander. Run cold water over the beans for a minute or so and then set them aside to drain.

TO MAKE THE DRESSING: In a small bowl, whisk together the vinegar, mustard, salt, and pepper. Slowly add the olive oil while continuing to whisk until the dressing is fully combined.

In a large serving bowl, combine the tomatoes, green beans, fresh peas, radishes, cucumber, arugula, basil, chives, and bread. Dress the salad and toss to combine.

MIMOSA SALAD

MAKES 4 SERVINGS

Salad

2 large eggs

1 large head butter lettuce

Dressing

1 tablespoon lemon juice

1 tablespoon champagne
vinegar

1 teaspoon Dijon mustard

1 tablespoon finely chopped
parsley

1 tablespoon finely chopped
chives

½ teaspoon salt

½ teaspoon pepper

⅓ cup/80 ml olive oil

A salad to be proud of . . . especially if you're a hen.

TO MAKE THE SALAD: Place a medium saucepan half full of water over high heat. When the water is at a full boil, use a spoon to gently lower the eggs into it, one at a time. Allow the eggs to boil for 10 minutes. Remove the saucepan from the heat and drain off the boiling water. Place the saucepan under the tap and run cold water over the eggs for several minutes until they have cooled enough to handle.

Take an egg and lightly tap both ends on the edge of the sink, then gently roll the egg along the counter to crack the shell. Hold the egg under cold running water while you peel off the shell. Once it has been removed, give the egg a little shake to remove any excess water and place it on a cutting board. Repeat with the remaining egg.

Cut each egg in half and remove the egg yolk. Use your hands to crumble the egg yolks into a small bowl. Finely chop the remaining egg whites and place them in another bowl. Chill the egg yolks and whites, covered, in the refrigerator while you prepare the rest of the salad.

Remove any wilted or damaged leaves from the butter lettuce. Cut the root off the bottom of the head and gently release each leaf. Fill the sink with cool water and submerge the leaves. Use your hands to give them a good swirl to remove any dirt or bugs from the garden (don't cringe . . . it happens). Drain the sink and repeat for a final rinse. (Normally I suggest using a salad spinner to wash greens, but I want to maintain the full leaves of the lettuce for assembling the salad, so I do it this way instead.) Lift the leaves from the water and give them a very gentle shake to remove any excess water. Then place them in a single layer on clean tea towels or paper towels and loosely roll the leaves up to dry.

TO MAKE THE DRESSING: In a small bowl, whisk together the lemon juice, vinegar, mustard, parsley, chives, salt, and pepper. Continue to whisk while slowly adding the olive oil until fully combined.

Place the lettuce leaves in a large serving bowl and use two large spoons or a set of salad tongs to toss with the dressing. Arrange the dressed leaves on a serving platter in concentric circles that slightly overlap. Sprinkle the chopped egg whites over the leaves and then top with the crumbled egg yolks. Sprinkle the eggs with a little more salt and pepper to serve.

POTATO & GREEN BEAN SALAD WITH HERB DRESSING

MAKES 4 TO 6 SERVINGS

Salad

¼ cup/60 ml white wine

1 tablespoon grainy Dijon
mustard

1 teaspoon salt

½ teaspoon pepper

1½ pounds/680 g Yukon Gold
potatoes, peeled and halved

8 oz/227 g green beans, ends
trimmed

Zest of 1 lemon

Dressing

1 tablespoon finely chopped
chives

1 tablespoon finely chopped
fresh dill

1 tablespoon finely chopped
fresh parsley

1 tablespoon finely chopped
fresh rosemary

1 tablespoon finely chopped
fresh mint

3 tablespoons lemon juice

½ teaspoon salt

½ teaspoon pepper

½ cup/125 ml olive oil

This salad really demonstrates how even the humblest of ingredients will shine when freshly picked from the garden and simply prepared.

TO MAKE THE SALAD: Place the white wine, mustard, salt, and pepper in a large mixing bowl and whisk to combine. Set aside.

TO MAKE THE DRESSING: Place the chives, dill, parsley, rosemary, mint, lemon juice, salt, and pepper in a small bowl and whisk to combine. Continue whisking while slowly adding the olive oil until fully combined. Set aside.

Place the prepared potatoes in a large pot of salted water over high heat. Bring to a boil, then reduce the heat to a simmer and allow them to cook until just fork tender, about 15 minutes. Drain the potatoes in a colander and allow to rest for a couple of minutes with a tea towel over the top. This will help to absorb the excess moisture and steam.

Add the potatoes to the mixing bowl and use a large spoon to gently toss them in the wine and mustard.

Bring a large pot of salted water to a boil over high heat. Gently lower the trimmed green beans into the boiling water and allow them to cook for 3 to 4 minutes, until just tender and bright green. Remove the beans from the heat and drain off the water.

Use a large spoon to toss the warm green beans with half of the prepared dressing and then transfer them to a shallow serving bowl. Toss the potatoes with the remaining dressing and place them atop the green beans. Zest the lemon over the salad and finish with another sprinkle of salt and pepper.

KALE SALAD WITH PECORINO, CRANBERRIES, APPLE & ALMONDS

Salad

2 bunches Tuscan kale

1 tablespoon olive oil

1 handful sliced almonds
   with skin

¼ teaspoon salt

1 cup/85 g grated pecorino
   cheese (see Note)

1 handful dried cranberries

1 large apple, cut into
   ½-inch/1.25 cm chunks

Dressing

¼ cup/60 ml lemon juice

1 tablespoon Dijon mustard

½ teaspoon salt

¼ teaspoon pepper

½ cup/125 ml olive oil

Everyone seems to have a version of this salad and for good reason: it's bloody fantastic. My favorite thing about this recipe is how well the dressed kale keeps. So well in fact, I often make the whole recipe just for Paul and me and save the leftovers for my lunch over the next couple of days. I prefer to make this salad with Tuscan kale, also known as lacinato, dinosaur, or black kale, as it is a little more tender than traditional curly kale.

TO MAKE THE SALAD: Remove the spines from the kale: I like to do this by holding each leaf by the stem with one hand and using the other hand to pull down with a finger on either side of the spine, from bottom to top. (Work fast and forcefully, and you'll be through the pile of leaves in no time.) Stack up the spineless leaves, roll them together, and chop them finely. Wash the chopped leaves in a salad spinner and place in a large bowl.

In a small frying pan over medium heat, place 1 tablespoon olive oil. Add the sliced almonds and stir to combine. Continue to cook until the almonds have lightly toasted. Keep a close eye on them as they can burn easily. Remove from the heat and place on a plate lined with paper towel. Sprinkle with the salt and set aside to cool.

Add the grated pecorino, dried cranberries, chopped apple, and toasted almonds to the bowl with the chopped kale.

TO MAKE THE DRESSING: In a small bowl, whisk together the lemon juice, mustard, salt, and pepper. Slowly whisk in the olive oil until well combined.

Pour the dressing over the salad and toss well to coat everything. Allow the salad to sit, dressed, for about 30 minutes before serving. This helps to soften the kale a smidge.

NOTE: *I like to grate my cheese in my blender. It sounds surprising, but it is so fast and creates a lovely fine grate perfect for sprinkling. Any extra I place in a container in the freezer for later use.*

SIMPLE GREENS WITH FRESH HERBS

MAKES 4 SERVINGS

Salad

2 small heads butter lettuce

1 tablespoon finely chopped
  fresh chives

1 tablespoon finely chopped
  fresh basil

1 tablespoon finely chopped
  fresh dill

1 tablespoon finely chopped
  fresh mint

Chive blossoms, for garnish
  (optional)

Dressing

3 tablespoons champagne
  vinegar

1 tablespoon Dijon mustard

1 teaspoon salt

½ teaspoon pepper

½ cup/125 ml olive oil

The inspiration for this salad came from a near perfect meal I once enjoyed with my daughter, India, at the restaurant Via Carota in NYC. While the taste was perfection, the real takeaway for me was the beautiful and delicate way they stacked the leaves. I love the impressive presentation it creates, and I think it's worth the effort (but if you are pressed for time, you can always just toss it all together as you would a regular salad).

TO MAKE THE SALAD: Remove any wilted or damaged leaves from the butter lettuce. Cut the root off the bottom of each head and gently release each leaf. Fill the sink with cool water and submerge the leaves. Use your hands to give them a good swirl to remove any dirt or bugs from the garden. Drain the sink and repeat for a final rinse. (Normally I suggest using a salad spinner to wash greens, but I want to maintain the full leaves of the lettuce for assembling the salad so I do it this way instead.) Lift the leaves from the water and give them a very gentle shake to remove any excess water. Then place them in a single layer on clean tea towels or paper towels and loosely roll the leaves up to dry.

In a small bowl, gently toss the chives, basil, dill, and mint together (this makes sprinkling easier).

TO MAKE THE DRESSING: In a small bowl, whisk the vinegar, mustard, salt, and pepper to combine. Slowly add the olive oil in a steady stream while continuing to whisk until fully combined.

In a large serving bowl or across four salad plates, place a small stack of the washed leaves. Sprinkle with the fresh herbs and a drizzle of dressing. Continue to repeat this step until you have achieved a lovely high stack of leaves smothered in herbs and dressing. Best served promptly, as butter lettuce is very tender.

CUCUMBER, CANTALOUPE & BLOOD ORANGE SALAD
WITH FETA & MINT

MAKES 4 TO 6 SERVINGS

Dressing

1 tablespoon red wine vinegar

½ teaspoon sugar

1 teaspoon salt

½ teaspoon pepper

3 tablespoons olive oil

Salad

½ large cantaloupe, peeled, seeds removed, and cut into ½-inch/1.25 cm slices

2 blood oranges, zested and then peeled and cut into ½-inch/1.25 cm segments (see page 85 for how to properly segment citrus)

1 small English cucumber, cut into 2-inch/5 cm chunks on random diagonals

3 to 4 radishes, thinly sliced

1 handful fresh mint leaves, roughly torn

½ teaspoon chili flakes

¼ cup/30 g crumbled feta cheese

1 handful fresh basil leaves, roughly torn (a mix of red and green basil is lovely)

The secret to this salad is finding the freshest, juiciest cantaloupe you can get your hands on. Hopefully you won't have to search any farther than your own garden. If that's not the case, not to worry, because homegrown cucumber and fresh mint are pretty special too!

TO MAKE THE DRESSING: In a small bowl, whisk together the vinegar, sugar, salt, and pepper. Continue to whisk while you slowly add the olive oil.

TO MAKE THE SALAD: Place the cantaloupe slices randomly on a large serving platter. Add the orange slices, cucumber pieces, and radish slices, again placing them randomly across the platter to create a pleasing balance to the eye.

Sprinkle with torn mint leaves, chili flakes, and feta cheese.

Drizzle the salad with the dressing and top with the torn basil and orange zest to serve.

TWO-THIRDS LIFE SIZE

PEAR VARIETIES

1. 'BERGAMOTTE D'ESPÉREN' 2. 'PACKHAM'S TRIUMPH'
3. 'DURONDEAU' 4. 'OLIVIER DE SERRES' 5. 'PASSE CRASANNE'

59

CUCUMBER & PRAWN NOODLE SALAD

MAKES 4 SERVINGS

Salad

1 large English cucumber
(or several little guys)

½ teaspoon salt

6 radishes

1 pound/454 g fresh prawns
(frozen is fine too),
washed and peeled

1 package (9.5 oz/269 g)
udon noodles (or the
noodles of your choice),
cooked and drained

Dressing

½ cup/125 ml rice vinegar

3 tablespoons sugar

½ teaspoon salt

1 teaspoon soy sauce

1 teaspoon peeled and finely
grated fresh ginger

1 tablespoon finely chopped
fresh chives

Prawn Rub

½ teaspoon ground ginger

½ teaspoon paprika

¼ teaspoon cayenne

½ teaspoon chili powder

½ teaspoon salt

1½ teaspoons lime juice

1 teaspoon sesame oil

Zest of 1 lime

When trying to come up with new ways to use up all the cucumbers fast appearing in my garden, I took inspiration from my favorite date night. It always involves Paul, two seats at our favorite Japanese restaurant, and a bottle of wine. We like to start our meal with a refreshing sunomono salad, a tangy little noodle dish topped with cucumbers and fresh shrimp. I upped the ante a smidge for this recipe with spicy prawns, and made it generous enough to serve four, because double dates are fun too.

TO MAKE THE SALAD: Using a sharp knife or mandoline (I always prefer the mandoline), thinly slice the cucumber, transfer to a small bowl, and sprinkle with the salt. This helps remove extra liquid from the cucumber, which will help keep them crunchy. Leave them to sit while you carry on with the recipe.

Wash and dry the radishes, remove and discard their tops, and use the same knife or mandoline to thinly slice the radishes. Set them aside in another bowl.

TO MAKE THE DRESSING: In a small bowl, whisk together the vinegar, sugar, salt, soy sauce, grated ginger, and chives. Set aside.

TO MAKE THE PRAWN RUB: In a medium bowl, combine the ground ginger, paprika, cayenne, chili powder, salt, lime juice, and sesame oil and use a spoon to stir the mixture until a paste forms. Place the peeled prawns in the bowl and gently toss to coat them with the rub. Set aside while you prepare the rest of the salad.

Prepare the noodles according to the package instructions. When just cooked, drain the noodles in a colander and then rinse with cold water. Drain them well again. Transfer the noodles to a large bowl and add half of the dressing. Use a large fork or tongs to toss the noodles to fully coat them in the dressing.

Position a rack near the top of the oven and turn the broiler on high. Line a baking sheet with parchment paper.

Pour off any excess liquid that may have accumulated from the cucumbers and then toss them in the remaining dressing.

Continued

To Serve

Sprinkle of finely chopped chives

Sprinkle of toasted sesame seeds

Salt and pepper

Sprinkle of roughly torn cilantro leaves

Squeeze of lime

Spread the prawns across the prepared baking sheet and place them under the hot broiler for 2 to 3 minutes. Remove from the oven and use a spatula to turn the prawns. Place them back in the oven for just a minute, until done; they cook very quickly so keep a close watch.

TO SERVE: Use a pair of tongs to transfer the noodles to a serving platter. Top them with the cucumbers and then the radishes. Sprinkle with the chives, sesame seeds, and a good grind of salt and pepper. Place the warm prawns atop the radishes and sprinkle the cilantro, a bit more salt and pepper, and a squeeze of lime.

ARUGULA SALAD WITH FENNEL & GRAPEFRUIT

MAKES 4 TO 6 SERVINGS

Salad

1 large pink grapefruit

3 big handfuls arugula,
  washed and dried

1 fennel bulb, thinly sliced

1 small English cucumber, cut
  into ½-inch/1.25 cm cubes

1 avocado, pitted and cut into
  1-inch/2.5 cm cubes

1 handful shelled pistachios,
  roughly chopped

Dressing

1 tablespoon white wine
  vinegar

1 teaspoon honey

½ teaspoon salt

½ teaspoon pepper

3 tablespoons olive oil

If you made it this far in life without knowing how to properly segment a piece of citrus, I applaud you. You are clearly a survivor. A survivor who has left a trail of crudely cut oranges and grapefruits in their wake, but hey, you're alive.

TO MAKE THE SALAD: On a clean cutting board, using a sharp knife, carefully cut off the top and bottom of the grapefruit. Stand the grapefruit up on one flat end. Cut the remaining peel off in sections by cutting down, from top to bottom. Continue until you have removed all the peel and membrane from the outer flesh of the grapefruit. Trim off any remaining bits of pith. Hold the grapefruit in one hand and use the knife to carefully cut between a segment and the membrane, slicing just until you are near the center of the fruit. Turn the edge of the knife just slightly and pull back to remove the segment from the balance of the membrane covering it. Repeat with the next segment, working your way all around the grapefruit (this life skill may take a little practice, but it is so worth the effort in the end).

TO MAKE THE DRESSING: In a small bowl, whisk together the vinegar, honey, salt, and pepper. Continue to whisk while slowly adding the olive oil until fully combined.

In a large serving bowl or deep platter, combine the arugula, fennel, cucumber, and avocado. Drizzle with dressing and toss to combine.

Top the greens with the grapefruit segments and sprinkle with the pistachios to serve.

BEET, BLACKBERRY & BUCKWHEAT SALAD

MAKES 4 SERVINGS

Salad

1 large or 2 medium beets

Olive oil, for drizzling

1 teaspoon salt

½ teaspoon pepper

1 handful hazelnuts

½ cup/85 g dried buckwheat

1 cup/150 g fresh blackberries

1 big handful fresh mint leaves,
   roughly torn

1 cup/250 ml labneh or plain
   Greek yogurt

Lemon zest, to serve

Dressing

1 tablespoon red wine vinegar

1 teaspoon dark brown sugar

½ teaspoon salt

3 tablespoons olive oil

I don't so much "grow" blackberries as "gather" them. Just as I like to travel with clippers in the glove box for spontaneous roadside floral heists, I find it an equally good idea to bring along a little pail when walking the dog during berry season. You never know when you might avail yourself of a random blackberry bush.

TO MAKE THE SALAD: Preheat the oven to 400°F/200°C. Rinse any dirt or debris off the beets and trim the tops and bottoms. Place the beets on a sheet of foil, drizzle with a little olive oil, and sprinkle with half of the salt and the pepper. Wrap them inside the foil and place directly on the oven rack to roast until fork tender, approximately 45 minutes.

Place the hazelnuts on a baking sheet or small baking pan and pop in the oven with the beets for 5 minutes, until they are lightly roasted and fragrant. Remove the baking sheet from the oven and allow the nuts to sit until they are cool enough to roughly chop. Don't worry about removing their skins; I like the added color they provide.

Remove the beets from the oven and set aside until they are cool enough to handle. Remove the skins of the beets and cut into 1-inch/2.5 cm pieces. Transfer the cut beets to a large bowl.

Fill a small saucepan with 1 cup/250 ml of water, the buckwheat, and the remaining ½ teaspoon salt. Place the pot over high heat and bring to a boil. Reduce the heat to a simmer, put the lid on, and allow the buckwheat to cook for about 10 minutes. Turn off the heat. Lift the lid, place a clean folded tea towel across the top of the pot, and replace the lid. Allow the buckwheat to steam for about 5 minutes more. Remove the lid and fluff the buckwheat with a fork.

Set the pot aside until the buckwheat has cooled and then add it to the beets.

Add the chopped nuts, blackberries, and torn mint to the bowl. Season with salt and pepper to taste and using a large spoon, toss to combine.

TO MAKE THE DRESSING: In a small bowl, whisk together the vinegar, brown sugar, and salt. Slowly add the olive oil while continuing to whisk until well combined. Dress the salad and toss it all again.

Use a spoon to spread the labneh or Greek yogurt across the bottom of a large serving platter. Top with the salad and sprinkle with lemon zest to serve.

WARM CABBAGE SLAW WITH APPLES & FENNEL

MAKES 4 TO 6 SERVINGS

1 handful walnuts

¼ cup/40 g golden raisins

¼ cup/60 ml dark rum

1 large Granny Smith apple,
    cut in half with core and
    seeds removed, thinly sliced

1 teaspoon ground cardamom

1 teaspoon sugar

2 tablespoons butter

2 tablespoons olive oil

2 small leeks, white and
    light green parts only,
    finely chopped

1 teaspoon mustard seeds

1 teaspoon anise seeds

1 teaspoon salt

1 teaspoon pepper

1 small savoy cabbage, cut into
    1-inch/2.5 cm wedges

1 medium fennel bulb, cut into
    ½-inch/1.25 cm wedges
    (save the fronds for garnish)

1 tablespoon finely chopped
    fresh parsley

Sprinkling of fennel fronds

Zest of lemon

I love this dish for its combination of crunchy bits and chewy bits all wrapped up in warmth, making it a perfect side dish once the weather starts to cool come fall.

Preheat the oven to 375°F/190°C. Place the walnuts on a baking sheet and bake for 4 to 6 minutes, until toasted and fragrant. Allow the nuts to rest until cool enough to handle and then roughly chop. Set aside.

Place the raisins and rum in a small saucepan over medium-high heat. Bring the rum to a boil, turn off the heat, and leave the raisins to soak in the rum.

Place the sliced apple in a small bowl with the cardamom and sugar and toss to evenly coat all the pieces. Set aside.

In a large frying pan, melt the butter and olive oil over medium-high heat. Add the leeks, mustard seeds, anise seeds, salt, and pepper, and continue to cook until the leeks are soft and just starting to brown, 5 to 7 minutes. Stir the leeks with a wooden spoon and adjust the heat as needed to prevent burning.

Add the cabbage and fennel to the pan and use the wooden spoon to stir them with the leeks and seasoning. Continue cooking until the cabbage has begun to wilt and the fennel is softening. Place the lid on the pan and continue cooking for about 15 minutes, making sure to lift the lid every 5 minutes or so and give it a good stir to prevent any burning.

Once the cabbage is starting to brown and caramelize, add the apple slices, stir again to combine, and continue cooking with the lid on for about 5 more minutes.

Take the lid off the pan and add the raisins and rum and a little more salt to taste. The apples should be just starting to soften but still have some crunch.

To serve, spoon the warm cabbage slaw onto a serving platter or bowl and sprinkle with the parsley, chopped walnuts, fennel fronds, and lemon zest. Season with more salt and pepper to taste.

ZUCCHINI NOODLE SALAD

MAKES 4 SERVINGS

Salad

1 package (9.5 oz/269 g)
  dried soba noodles

1 tablespoon olive oil, plus
  more for drizzling noodles

1 red Thai chili pepper, finely
  chopped with seeds

2 large handfuls shredded
  napa cabbage

1 red pepper, chopped in
  ½-inch/1.25 cm pieces

2 stalks celery, thinly sliced

2 medium zucchini, spiralized
  (see Note)

2 tablespoons dry-roasted and
  salted peanuts, roughly
  chopped

2 tablespoons finely chopped
  cilantro

1 green onion, finely chopped

1 lime, quartered

Dressing

3 tablespoons peanut butter

2 tablespoons soy sauce

1 tablespoon fresh lime juice

1 tablespoon freshly grated
  ginger

2 tablespoons honey

2 tablespoons sesame oil

2 tablespoons rice wine vinegar

I don't often write recipes that require odd pieces of equipment, as I know that can be a little annoying to the reader. But a spiralizer is one of those items that I am going to encourage you to buy. They're low on cost and high on fun, not to mention all the health benefits you'll get from the piles and piles of veggie noodles you'll make!

TO MAKE THE SALAD: Cook the noodles as instructed on the package, making sure to save ¼ cup/60 ml of the cooking water before draining. Run the noodles under cool water, drain again, and set aside. You can toss the noodles with a drizzle of olive oil to keep them from all sticking together in a clump while you are preparing the rest of the dish.

TO MAKE THE DRESSING: In a medium bowl, combine the peanut butter, soy sauce, lime juice, ginger, honey, sesame oil, and vinegar and whisk to fully combine.

Heat 1 tablespoon olive oil in a large frying pan over medium-high heat. Add the chili pepper, cabbage, red pepper, and celery and continue to cook until they have started to soften, 7 to 10 minutes.

Add the noodles, dressing, and spiralized zucchini and stir to combine. If you find that you'd like the salad to be a little saucier, add some of the reserved noodle water until it reaches the desired consistency.

Use a pair of tongs or pasta server to scoop the noodles into shallow bowls and top each serving with a sprinkle of peanuts, cilantro, and green onion with a wedge of lime on the side for squeezing.

NOTE: *If you don't own a spiralizer and your grocery store doesn't sell spiralized zucchini premade, you can grate the zucchini on a box grater or with a food processor. While the overall taste will be the same, it won't look quite as appealing as the long noodles will.*

TOMATO, BACON & BLUE CHEESE SALAD

MAKES 4 TO 6 SERVINGS

Salad

3 slices thick-cut bacon

1½ pounds/680 g grape and cherry tomatoes, any combination, washed and cut in half

1 teaspoon fresh thyme leaves

½ teaspoon finely chopped fresh rosemary

1 teaspoon finely chopped fresh oregano

1 teaspoon fennel seeds, lightly chopped

½ cup/55 g crumbled blue cheese

1 teaspoon finely chopped fresh chives

Dressing

1 tablespoon red wine vinegar

1 teaspoon Dijon mustard

½ teaspoon salt

½ teaspoon pepper

3 tablespoons olive oil

All the best parts of a BLT sandwich in one bowl. You can make this salad at any time of year, but it is best when made with tomatoes picked fresh off the vine.

TO MAKE THE SALAD: Preheat the oven to 375°F/190°C. Line a baking sheet with parchment paper. Lay the three slices of bacon side by side on the prepared baking sheet and bake for 15 to 20 minutes, using tongs to turn the bacon over at the halfway point, until the bacon is cooked through and crispy around the edges. Once done, remove from the oven and use the tongs to transfer the bacon to some paper towel to absorb the excess oil, then cut into 1-inch/2.5 cm pieces.

Place the tomato halves, thyme, rosemary, oregano, fennel seeds, and bacon pieces in a large serving bowl.

TO MAKE THE DRESSING: In a small bowl, whisk together the vinegar, mustard, salt, and pepper. Continue to whisk while slowly adding the olive oil until fully combined.

Pour the dressing over the tomato mixture and use two large spoons to toss the salad together. Sprinkle with blue cheese and chopped chives and serve.

FENNEL COLESLAW WITH CURRIED CASHEWS

MAKES 4 TO 6 SERVINGS

Dressing

⅓ cup/80 ml mayonnaise

1 tablespoon apple cider vinegar

1 teaspoon honey Dijon mustard

1 teaspoon honey

1 teaspoon salt

½ teaspoon pepper

Salad

1 small fennel bulb, finely sliced, fronds removed

2 big handfuls finely sliced napa cabbage

1 big handful finely sliced radicchio

1 big handful peeled and grated carrot

1 handful Curried Cashews (page 96), roughly chopped

1 green apple, washed and cut into 1-inch/2.5 cm cubes

1 handful golden raisins

1 teaspoon fennel seeds

2 teaspoons finely chopped fresh parsley

2 teaspoons finely chopped fresh chives

1 teaspoon finely chopped fresh mint

1 teaspoon finely chopped fresh dill

1 tablespoon fresh cilantro leaves, roughly torn

This salad is a nice alternative to the standard idea of coleslaw we all know. It works well as a side with grilled fish or burgers, but I'm also just as happy to eat a bowl of it on its own for lunch. The curried cashews in this recipe couldn't be easier or quicker to make! They are a delicious little nibble to serve with drinks any time of year but also work just as well sprinkled on almost any salad when you want to add a little crunch. If you don't have time to whip up a batch of curried cashews, you can always substitute roasted almonds.

TO MAKE THE DRESSING: In a small bowl, whisk together the mayonnaise, vinegar, mustard, honey, salt, and pepper until well combined.

TO MAKE THE SALAD: Place the sliced fennel, napa cabbage, and radicchio in a large bowl. Add the grated carrot, half of the chopped curried cashews, and the apple cubes, raisins, fennel seeds, parsley, chives, mint, and dill.

Use two large spoons or tongs to toss and combine. Add the dressing and toss again. Transfer the salad to a shallow serving bowl and sprinkle with the remaining nuts and cilantro leaves to serve.

Continued

CURRIED CASHEWS

MAKES 2 CUPS/280 G

1 teaspoon butter, melted
1 teaspoon dark brown sugar
1 teaspoon curry powder
1 teaspoon salt
2 cups/280 g cashews

In a medium bowl, whisk together the melted butter, brown sugar, curry powder, and salt until well combined.

Preheat the oven to 350°F/180°C. Line a baking sheet with parchment paper and spread the cashews across it. Place in the oven and roast until the cashews are fragrant and starting to turn a golden brown, 5 to 8 minutes. Make sure to give the pan a good shake at the halfway point for even roasting.

Remove the nuts from the oven and immediately transfer them to the bowl with the curry mixture. Do this by carefully lifting both sides of the parchment paper to create a little chute and pour them in the bowl. Use a large spoon to toss the nuts and coat them in the curry butter. Allow the nuts to cool until they are dry to the touch, 10 to 15 minutes, before serving. The nuts will keep in an airtight container for up to 1 week.

ARUGULA SALAD WITH WARM FIGS & CRISPY PROSCIUTTO

Salad

4 thin slices prosciutto

4 fresh figs, sliced in half

2 teaspoons sugar

4 large handfuls arugula, washed and dried

½ cup/50 g parmesan shavings

Dressing

1 tablespoon balsamic vinegar

2 teaspoons honey

½ teaspoon salt

½ teaspoon pepper

3 tablespoons olive oil

Homegrown figs are truly something to be proud of, but I'm not one of those lucky people who have their own fig tree. However, I've heard that covert operations under the darkness of night can yield a nice little bounty from one's neighbors.

TO MAKE THE SALAD: Preheat the oven to 350°F/180°C. Line a baking sheet with parchment paper and lay the slices of prosciutto across it. Bake for 8 to 10 minutes, until the prosciutto is mostly crispy. Keep an eye on it as you don't want it to burn. Remove from the oven and transfer the prosciutto to a wire rack to cool completely.

Sprinkle the cut side of each fig half with sugar and lay face down in a frying pan over medium-high heat. Allow the figs to cook until the sugar starts to bubble, about 5 minutes. Turn the figs over and continue to cook until they just start to soften their shape a little, 3 to 5 minutes more. Remove from the heat.

TO MAKE THE DRESSING: In a small bowl, place the vinegar, honey, salt, and pepper and whisk to combine. Continue to whisk while you slowly add the olive oil to the bowl, until fully combined.

Place the arugula in a large salad bowl with the dressing and toss to combine.

Divide the salad between four plates and use your hands to crush and crumble one piece of prosciutto atop each serving. Sprinkle with parmesan shavings and add two halves of the warm figs to each plate to serve. You can also assemble the salad on a single serving platter.

MAINS

RED PEPPER BISQUE WITH CRAB

MAKES 6 SERVINGS

1 tablespoon butter

1 tablespoon olive oil

2 small leeks, light green and
white parts only, cut in
half and thinly sliced

1 teaspoon Old Bay seasoning

1 red Thai chili pepper, finely
sliced with seeds

1 teaspoon salt

½ teaspoon ground pepper

4 red peppers, cut into
½-inch/1.25 cm pieces

4 medium tomatoes, seeds
removed, cut into
½-inch/1.25 cm pieces

4 cups/1 liter chicken stock

1 cup/250 ml coconut milk

Zest of 1 lemon

8 oz/227 g lump crab meat,
rinsed and drained

2 tablespoons finely chopped
cilantro

This might be my favorite recipe in the whole book. Just do me a favor and don't tell the other recipes I said so, or all hell will break loose. It's as versatile as it is delicious: It makes a wonderful starter for a special meal, or a lighter dinner or lunch served on its own. If you're not a fan of crab, you can omit it and simply garnish as instructed or add a dollop of Olive Tapenade (page 197).

In a large pot over medium-high heat, melt the butter and olive oil. Add the leeks, Old Bay seasoning, red chili pepper, salt, and pepper and stir to combine. Turn the heat down to medium and allow the leeks to cook, stirring occasionally, until they are very tender, 5 to 8 minutes.

Add the chopped red peppers and tomatoes and continue to cook until the peppers soften and the tomatoes begin to break down, approximately another 5 to 8 minutes.

Add the chicken stock and bring the entire pot to a low boil for a few minutes.

Take the pot off the heat and allow the soup to cool slightly before transferring it in two or three batches to your blender to puree (you'll need a secondary mixing bowl to hold the pureed soup while you finish the other batches). If you are using an immersion blender, you can puree the soup right in the pot, but you won't get as smooth a finish.

Return the soup to the pot over medium heat and stir in the coconut milk and lemon zest.

To serve, place about a handful of crab meat in the center of each bowl. Carefully ladle the soup around the mound of crab and sprinkle with a teaspoon of the chopped cilantro.

You can make the soup through to the pureeing in advance and store, covered, in the refrigerator for up to 3 days or in the freezer for up to 3 months. Simply defrost, reheat, and add the coconut milk and lemon zest.

ZUCCHINI RICOTTA TART

MAKES 4 TO 6 SERVINGS

10 × 14-inch/25 × 35 cm piece
    puff pastry, about
    ⅛ inch/3 mm thick

1 tablespoon butter

2 large shallots, finely chopped

Sprinkle of sugar

Sprinkle plus ½ teaspoon salt

Sprinkle plus ½ teaspoon
    pepper

1½ cups/374 g ricotta cheese

¼ cup/43 g goat cheese

Zest of 1 lemon

1 tablespoon lemon juice

2 medium zucchini, sliced
    ⅛ inch/3 mm thick

1 tablespoon olive oil

1 tablespoon fresh thyme leaves

1 egg, lightly beaten

I love a quality shortcut. And by quality, I mean that whatever the time-saver, it won't compromise the finished product. A cake mix might be fast, but the cake is never going to be as good as one made from scratch. Good puff pastry, however, can be found in the freezer section of your grocer and will save you tons of time and effort.

If you're lucky enough to find the brand Dufour, grab it! It does cost a little more, but that is because, unlike its competitors' products, it's made with real butter. Another huge plus is the size of the sheet. When unfolded, it's the perfect dimensions for this tart. No rolling necessary. This, people, is the very definition of a quality shortcut! You're welcome.

Preheat the oven to 400°F/200°C. Line a baking sheet with parchment paper. Place the puff pastry on the baking sheet and use a small knife to score a 1-inch/2.5 cm border around the edge, making sure not to cut right through the pastry. This will create a lovely puffed crust for the tart.

In a small frying pan over medium-high heat, melt the butter. Add the chopped shallots, a sprinkle of sugar, and a dash of salt and pepper. Cook the shallots until they begin to brown, adjusting the heat as you go to ensure they don't burn. Continue to cook them until they are very soft and evenly golden brown, about 10 minutes. Set aside to cool.

In a food processor, place the ricotta cheese, goat cheese, lemon zest, lemon juice, and ½ teaspoon each of salt and pepper. Blend on high until creamy and smooth.

Place the zucchini slices in one layer across several sheets of paper towel. Sprinkle with salt and allow them to sit for several minutes to release some of their moisture. Lay more paper towel atop the slices and gently roll them up. Give them a little squeeze to again remove as much extra liquid as possible and set aside.

Spread the caramelized shallots evenly within the border of the puff pastry, top with the whipped ricotta and then lay the zucchini slices in overlapping rows on top.

Finish with a little more salt and pepper, a drizzle of olive oil, and a sprinkle of fresh thyme. Use a pastry brush to lightly coat the border with the beaten egg. Bake the tart for 25 to 30 minutes, until it is puffed and golden.

SAVORY DUTCH BABY

MAKES 4 SERVINGS

4 large eggs

¾ cup/180 ml whole milk

¾ cup/90 g all-purpose flour

½ teaspoon salt

½ teaspoon pepper

4 slices bacon, cut into
    1-inch/2.5 cm pieces

1 large handful cherry tomatoes

1 large handful fresh spinach

1 tablespoon butter

1 tablespoon finely chopped
    fresh parsley

1 tablespoon finely chopped
    fresh basil

½ cup/50 g freshly grated
    parmesan

An easy dish to bring together with rather impressive results. It is quite fun to stand around the oven door and watch the baby grow! Should you prefer a sweeter option, you can omit the bacon step and just use an extra tablespoon of butter in the pan when baking, then simply replace the tomatoes and herbs with fresh berries and a sprinkle of icing sugar.

Preheat the oven to 425°F/220°C.

In a small mixing bowl, whisk the eggs and milk. Continue whisking while sprinkling in the flour until fully combined. Add the salt and pepper and whisk again until a mostly smooth batter forms, but don't stress if there are a few little lumps.

In a medium-sized frying pan about 10 inches/25 cm in diameter, cook the bacon over medium-high heat until it has cooked through. Add the cherry tomatoes and allow them to cook until they are starting to color and some are just starting to burst, 5 to 7 minutes.

Place the spinach in a mixing bowl. Remove the pan from the heat. Use a large slotted spoon to transfer the bacon (keeping the drippings in the pan for later) and tomatoes to the bowl and toss to combine with the spinach until it has wilted. Set aside.

Add the butter to the same frying pan with bacon drippings and place it in the oven for about 3 to 5 minutes, until the butter has melted and the pan is very hot. Open the oven door, pull out the rack, and carefully pour the batter into the pan before closing the door again.

Bake for 20 to 25 minutes, until puffed and golden.

Remove the pan from the oven. Gently lift out the Dutch baby and place it on a serving plate. Spoon the bacon, tomatoes, and spinach into the center and sprinkle with parsley, basil, and parmesan to serve.

BEET RAVIOLI IN BROWN BUTTER & SAGE

MAKES 4 SERVINGS

Pasta

2 cups/240 g all-purpose flour

1 teaspoon salt

3 large eggs

Filling

3 medium beets

Olive oil

Sprinkle plus 1 teaspoon salt

Sprinkle plus ½ teaspoon pepper

¾ cup/185 g ricotta cheese

½ cup/50 g grated parmesan

1 tablespoon fresh thyme leaves

1 teaspoon lemon zest

Brown Butter & Sage

3 tablespoons Brown Butter (page 199)

4 fresh sage leaves

Squeeze of lemon

1 handful grated parmesan, plus a little more for sprinkling

While the idea of making your own ravioli might seem a little daunting at first, fear not; I've found that the secret to pretty much any task is breaking it down into smaller ones. For this recipe, the pasta and the filling can be prepared a day in advance, leaving only the rolling and assembly to tackle on the day itself. Before you know it, you'll be standing around with nothing to do.

TO MAKE THE PASTA: Place the flour on a clean work surface and create a well in the center. Sprinkle the salt around the edges and crack the eggs into the middle of the well. Use a fork to gently whisk the eggs while simultaneously pulling in flour from the edges of the well. When the dough becomes too thick to stir with a fork, use your finger to continue to work in the flour. Once the dough has mostly come together, begin to knead it. Continue to knead for about 10 minutes, until it is shiny and smooth.

Wrap the dough in plastic wrap and allow it to rest in the refrigerator for at least 1 hour or overnight. This will give the gluten that has developed a chance to relax, which will make rolling the pasta a lot easier on you.

TO MAKE THE FILLING: Preheat the oven to 400°F/200°C. Rinse any dirt or debris off the beets and trim the tops and bottoms, setting aside the tops for later.

Place the beets on a sheet of foil, drizzle with a little olive oil, and sprinkle with salt and pepper. Wrap them in the foil and place in the oven to roast until fork tender, approximately 45 minutes. Remove the beets from the oven and set them aside. Once they are cool enough to handle, remove and discard the skin of each beet.

Place the beets in a food processor. Blend until quite smooth. Add the beet tops, ricotta, parmesan, thyme, lemon zest, 1 teaspoon salt, and ½ teaspoon pepper to the food processor and blend until well combined.

Continued

TO ROLL THE DOUGH: Remove the dough from the refrigerator and cut it into four equal pieces. Work with one piece at a time, tightly wrapping the remaining pieces in plastic wrap so they don't dry out. If you have a pasta machine, follow the manufacturer's instructions for rolling and cutting the dough. If not, grab a rolling pin and carry on.

On a lightly floured work surface, roll the dough out to a very thin rectangular sheet, approximately 6 × 18 inches/15 × 46 cm and ⅟₃₂ inch/ 0.75 mm thick. Cut the sheet of pasta in half and set one piece to the side.

TO CREATE THE RAVIOLI: If you are using a ravioli tray (which would *definitely* be my chosen method for ease and efficiency), place one piece of pasta atop it, and fill each divot with 1 teaspoon of filling, then top with the other sheet of pasta. Run a rolling pin across the top to cut the ravioli out.

If you are working entirely by hand, simply place twelve dots of filling on one of the pasta sheets (it works well to create two rows of six), top with the remaining pasta sheet and use a pasta stamp (circular or square) to cut out each ravioli; if you don't have a stamp, you can use a circular cookie cutter or a knife and seal the edges with the tines of a fork. (This will take forever and you will probably hate me and never make pasta again, so please buy a tray or stamps so we can still be friends. And while we are on the subject, the pasta attachment for KitchenAid mixers is a game changer, so do consider investing in that too!)

Place the ravioli on a baking sheet or platter and repeat the process with the remaining pasta dough.

TO COOK THE RAVIOLI: Bring a large pot of heavily salted water to a boil over high heat. Once boiling, add the ravioli and allow it to cook until just tender and beginning to float, 3 to 4 minutes. Set aside ¼ cup/60 ml of pasta water and then drain the ravioli in a colander.

TO MAKE THE BROWN BUTTER AND SAGE: In a large saucepan, prepare the brown butter (see the recipe on page 199). Once the butter has browned, add the sage leaves and a squeeze of lemon to the pan. Continue to cook until the sage leaves just begin to crisp. This happens pretty quickly, so do keep an eye on them. Add the cooked ravioli to the butter and gently toss to coat them. Add the handful of grated parmesan and toss again. You can add a little of the reserved pasta water now if it doesn't feel quite saucy enough.

Divide the ravioli across four pasta bowls (or two; wink, wink, nudge, nudge) and top with a grind of pepper and extra sprinkle of parmesan to serve.

This ravioli, like most fresh pasta, will freeze well. To do so simply spread them across a baking sheet and pop them into the freezer. Once frozen, transfer them to a freezer bag for storage; they will keep frozen nicely for up to 3 months. There is no need to defrost them before cooking; just toss the frozen ravioli into the boiling water and prepare as instructed above.

WILTED GREENS TART

MAKES ONE 9-INCH/23 CM
TART, 6 SERVINGS

6 to 8 sheets phyllo pastry

½ cup/113 g butter, melted

2 tablespoons butter

1 shallot, peeled and finely diced

1 big handful kale, washed, spines removed, and roughly torn

1 big handful fresh spinach, washed

1 big handful fresh arugula, washed

Sprinkle plus 1 teaspoon salt

Sprinkle plus ½ teaspoon pepper

½ cup/55 g crumbled feta cheese

4 large eggs

1 cup/250 ml whipping cream

Another wonderful way to use all those fresh greens from your garden. For those of you hesitant to make pastry, phyllo is your friend! I always have a box in the freezer for a variety of uses, but this tart shell is one of my favorites. Not only does it save tons of time, but there is also something rather lovely about the randomness of the folds and edges of the finished tart. If pie crust had a laid-back, easygoing cousin, this would be it.

Preheat the oven to 350°F/180°C.

Place a piece of phyllo on a clean work surface and use a pastry brush to gently coat it with some of the melted butter. Transfer this piece of phyllo into a 9-inch/23 cm quiche pan, carefully pushing it down to the bottom of the pan. Allow the excess to slightly hang over the edge of the pan. Repeat with the next sheet of phyllo, giving it a 10-degree turn every time you layer a piece. Don't worry if it tears; just paste it together with a brush of melted butter and carry on until you have completed the whole shell. Set aside.

Melt the 2 tablespoons of butter in a large frying pan over medium-high heat. Add the chopped shallot and cook until it is translucent and has started to soften. Add the kale, spinach, and arugula and continue to cook until all the greens are soft and wilted. Sprinkle with salt and pepper and place in the prepared shell.

Sprinkle the crumbled feta over the greens.

In a medium bowl, whisk together the eggs, cream, 1 teaspoon salt, and ½ teaspoon pepper and pour over the cheese and greens.

Bake on the center rack of the oven for 20 to 25 minutes, until the center is puffed and the phyllo is a lovely golden brown.

Remove the tart from the oven and allow it to cool slightly before removing it from the pan and placing it on a serving plate. It can be served warm or at room temperature.

The tart will keep, covered, in the refrigerator for several days.

POTATO PIZZA WITH MASCARPONE

MAKES ONE 10-INCH/
25 CM PIZZA

1 large Yukon Gold potato,
  washed and very thinly
  sliced

1 tablespoon olive oil, plus
  more for drizzling

1 tablespoon butter

1 medium onion, thinly sliced

1 ball Pizza Dough (page 120)

3 tablespoons mascarpone
  cheese

1 tablespoon fresh rosemary,
  finely chopped, plus more
  for sprinkling

½ teaspoon salt

½ teaspoon pepper

Freshly grated parmesan,
  for sprinkling

Oh sure, potatoes are a strange choice, but somehow pineapple makes sense? The potato or pineapple quandary just demonstrates that there really are no rules when dressing a pizza, so have a good look around your garden and get creative. Fresh-picked peas with ham, a mound of arugula atop prosciutto or zucchini, or ricotta and fresh herbs are just a few of the endless choices. Fortunately, my dough recipe makes enough for two pizzas, thereby allowing you to experiment with a new combo on the extra ball or to double up on the potato recipe to make two. If one pizza is all you need, simply wrap and freeze the extra dough ball for a later date. I learned to make the pizza dough on the next page while on vacation in Italy, and Paul and I both swear to this day it was the best pizza we have ever eaten. Of course, we were heavily under the influence of the Umbrian countryside and local wine, so it's a bloody miracle I can remember any of it.

Place a pizza stone on the middle rack of the oven and preheat to 500°F/260°C.

Place the thinly sliced potato (a handheld mandoline works beautifully for this) in a small mixing bowl and toss with the olive oil and a sprinkle of salt. Set the bowl aside for 5 to 10 minutes to allow the excess liquid to be pulled from the potatoes. Lay the sliced potatoes on a piece of paper towel and top and pat with another piece to help dry them.

Melt the butter in a medium frying pan set over medium-high heat. Add the thinly sliced onion (again, the handheld mandoline is the ideal tool for this job—if you don't own one, get one; you'll thank me later, I promise) and cook until the onions are turning a lovely dark brown and caramelized, about 10 minutes. Adjust the heat as necessary to avoid burning. Set aside.

Using your hands or a rolling pin on a lightly floured work surface, stretch the dough ball into a 10-inch/25 cm circle, being careful not to tear it or make holes. Transfer the pizza crust to a pizza peel or lightly floured rimless baking sheet (you need to be able to slide the dough onto the hot stone, so a pizza peel would be your best bet, and mine is nonstick, which makes it even easier!).

Using a small offset spatula, carefully spread the mascarpone cheese across the pizza crust, leaving a 1-inch/2.5 cm edge all around. Evenly distribute the caramelized onions across the cheese and then top with the chopped rosemary and then potato slices, partially overlapping them as you go.

Continued

Sprinkle with the salt and pepper and bake for about 10 minutes, until the crust is browning and the potatoes are tender and golden.

Remove the pizza from the oven and place on a cutting board. Drizzle with a little olive oil, a smidge more chopped rosemary, and some grated parmesan to serve.

PIZZA DOUGH

MAKES 2 BALLS OF
DOUGH, ENOUGH FOR TWO
10-INCH/25 CM PIZZAS

1 cup/250 ml warm water

2 teaspoons active dry yeast

2 cups/225 g "00" flour

⅓ cup/40 g all-purpose flour

1½ teaspoons salt

1 tablespoon olive oil

In a small bowl, place the warm water and yeast, stir to combine, and allow it to sit for several minutes until the yeast begins to bloom.

Place both flours and the salt in the bowl of a stand mixer fitted with the dough hook. Give it a couple of turns to combine.

With the mixer running on low, add the water and yeast and continue to beat until it is starting to come together. Add the olive oil and turn the mixer to high. Continue beating until the dough is fully combined and pulls away from the sides of the bowl, 5 to 7 minutes. (If you don't have a stand mixer, you can mix the dough in a bowl with a wooden spoon and then turn it out on a clean work surface to knead by hand until fully combined and able to form a smooth ball, about 10 minutes.)

Place the dough in a mixing bowl, cover with a clean tea towel or plastic wrap, and let it rise in a warm, draft-free spot on your counter until doubled in size, 1 to 2 hours.

Remove the towel and use your fist to punch the dough down to release any air inside. I personally prefer to allow my dough a second rise overnight in the refrigerator; this extra step really helps develop the flavor of the dough while also allowing the gluten to fully relax, making it much easier to shape and stretch. If you're not in a rush for your pizza, cover the bowl with plastic wrap again and allow it to rest in the refrigerator for up to 24 hours. Remove the dough from the refrigerator about an hour before shaping. Turn the dough out onto a lightly floured work surface. Divide the dough in half and shape each half into a ball.

If you want to use the dough immediately after the first rise, turn it out onto a lightly floured work surface. Divide the dough in half and shape each piece into a ball. Cover with a tea towel and allow the dough to rest for about 20 minutes before stretching and shaping for your pizza crust.

The dough will keep for a couple of days in the refrigerator or several months, well wrapped, in the freezer.

VEGETABLE CANNELLONI

MAKES 4 SERVINGS

1 medium zucchini, cut in
　1-inch/2.5 cm pieces

1 red pepper, seeds removed,
　cut in 1-inch/2.5 cm pieces

1 small red onion, peeled and
　chopped

1 small eggplant, peeled and
　cut in 1-inch/2.5 cm pieces

2 tablespoons olive oil

2 teaspoons Italian seasoning

1 teaspoon salt

½ teaspoon pepper

1 cup/262 g ricotta cheese

1 large egg

½ cup/50 g plus 2 tablespoons
　finely grated parmesan

Zest of 1 lemon

3 large handfuls fresh spinach

3½ cups/796 ml Roasted
　Tomato Sauce (page 193)
　or 1 can (28 fl oz/875 ml/
　794 g) plum tomatoes,
　crushed by hand (see Note)

10 Crepes (page 124 and
　see Note)

1 cup/115 g grated mozzarella

The next time you invite the UN over for dinner, make this dish. Italian enchiladas wrapped up in French crepes check a lot of boxes.

Preheat the oven to 400°F/200°C. Line a baking sheet with parchment paper.

In a large bowl, combine the zucchini, red pepper, red onion, and eggplant with the olive oil, Italian seasoning, salt, and pepper. Use a large spoon or your hands to gently toss all the veggies in the oil and seasoning.

Spread the vegetables across the prepared baking sheet and bake for 25 to 30 minutes, until they are fully roasted and beginning to brown. Remove from the oven and set them aside to cool slightly on the baking sheet slightly. Lower the oven temperature to 350°F/180°C.

Transfer the vegetables to the bowl of a food processor by lifting the piece of parchment on either side and tilting it over the bowl to create a chute for them to slide down. Put the lid on and pulse the processor a few times to start to chop up the vegetables. Add the ricotta, egg, ½ cup/43 g of the parmesan, and the lemon zest and pulse again to combine. Add the spinach and pulse until fully combined.

Fit a large piping bag with a large, plain tip and fill it with the vegetable ricotta mixture.

Spread 1 cup/250 ml of the tomato sauce in the bottom of a 9 × 13-inch/ 23 × 33 cm casserole dish.

Lay one crepe on a clean work surface or cutting board. Generously pipe a thick row of vegetable ricotta filling in the bottom half of the crepe by moving the piping tip horizontally from one side to the other and back again. Roll the crepe from the bottom up and then carefully place it in the casserole dish. Repeat with the remaining crepes until they are all snugly lined up.

Pour the balance of the tomato sauce over the cannelloni and then sprinkle with the mozzarella and remaining parmesan.

Continued

Bake for 25 to 30 minutes, until the sauce is bubbling and the cheese is turning a lovely golden brown. Remove the cannelloni from the oven and allow it to sit for 10 to 15 minutes before serving. The crepes are very tender, which makes serving a little challenging if the dish is screaming hot.

NOTE: *If using a can of plum tomatoes for this sauce, I like to empty the can into a bowl and crush each tomato by hand by giving them a good squeeze to break them down before using. You can always substitute regular pasta cannelloni shells if you don't have the time to make the crepes.*

CREPES

MAKES ABOUT 12 CREPES

1 cup/120 g all-purpose flour

½ teaspoon salt

1 large egg

1¾ cups/430 ml whole milk

2 tablespoons melted butter

In a medium bowl (or blender) place all the ingredients and whisk until you have a smooth, runny batter. If the batter is too thick, it won't run easily enough in the pan to create a thin crepe. You can always add a little more milk if you think it needs thinning.

In a nonstick frying pan over medium-high heat, spoon approximately ¼ cup/60 ml of batter into the center of the pan. Quickly tilt the pan in a circular motion and move the batter evenly around.

Allow the crepe to cook for 2 to 3 minutes, until the edges are starting to lift and the bottom is just starting to color. Use a metal spatula to help you lift the crepe and flip it over to briefly cook on the other side. Carefully remove the crepe from the pan and lay it on a platter or large plate. Repeat with the remaining batter.

NOTE: *This great basic recipe makes crepes that are just as delicious filled with roasted vegetables as they are with whipped cream and berries or ham and cheese or lemon and sugar or . . . Which leads me to my only piece of crepe advice: If you find yourself in Paris ordering a crepe from your favorite crepe stand on the Boulevard Saint-Germain, don't order a jambon crepe if you really want a jam crepe. Only do that if you want a ham crepe. Trust me, I know about these things.*

TOMATO GALETTE WITH OLIVE TAPENADE & BLACK PEPPER PASTRY

MAKES ONE 9-INCH/23 CM TART, 4 TO 6 SERVINGS

Black Pepper Pastry

1½ cups/180 g all-purpose flour

½ cup/50 g finely grated parmesan

1 teaspoon salt

1 teaspoon black pepper

¾ cup/170 g butter, chilled and cut into 1-inch/2.5 cm cubes

¼ cup/60 ml ice water

Tomato Galette

¼ cup/60 ml Olive Tapenade (page 197)

1 pound/454 g red or yellow cherry tomatoes

1 egg, lightly beaten

Parmesan for sprinkling

1 handful fresh basil leaves

Just as a fresh berry pie screams of summer, so too does this savory version of itself. And it's a perfect lunch or dinner with a simple salad and maybe a glass (or two) of rosé. Slice the pieces a little thinner and it makes for a pretty great appetizer as well.

TO MAKE THE PASTRY: Place the flour, parmesan, salt, and pepper in the bowl of a food processor fitted with the blade attachment. Pulse a couple of times to combine. Add the chilled cubed butter and continue to pulse until pea-sized crumbs begin to form.

With the food processor running, slowly add the ice water through the feed tube in a steady stream. As soon as the dough starts to come together, stop the machine. Remove the dough from the bowl and shape it into a disk. Wrap the disk in plastic wrap and chill in the refrigerator for at least 2 hours or overnight.

TO MAKE THE TOMATO GALETTE: Preheat the oven to 350°F/180°C. Line a baking sheet with parchment paper.

Remove the chilled disk of dough from the refrigerator and place it on a lightly floured work surface. Use a rolling pin to roll from the center of the dough out toward the edges, rotating the dough every few strokes to make sure it doesn't stick to the counter. Continue to roll until the pastry is about ⅛ inch/3 mm thick and 14 inches/35 cm in diameter.

Carefully fold the pastry in half and then in half again. Transfer the dough to the center of the prepared baking sheet and gently unfold it.

Use a small offset spatula or the back of a spoon to evenly spread the olive tapenade across the pastry in a circle, leaving a 2-inch/5 cm border all around for folding.

Spread the cherry tomatoes across the tapenade and then begin to fold the remaining pastry over on top of the tomatoes, making a tuck around the edge every 2 inches/5 cm or so. Continue until the galette is fully formed with a window on top exposing some of the tomatoes.

Continued

Use a pastry brush to coat the top and sides of the galette with the beaten egg.

Bake for 45 to 50 minutes, until the pastry is a lovely golden brown and the tomatoes are fully roasted and bubbling. Remove the galette from the oven and allow it to cool before slicing, as it will be pretty juicy when first baked.

Sprinkle the top of the galette with a little more grated parmesan and some fresh basil before serving.

SPINACH PESTO ON PASTA

MAKES 4 SERVINGS

Spinach Pesto

2 cloves garlic, peeled

1 teaspoon olive oil

1 big handful walnuts

3 handfuls fresh spinach, washed and mostly dried

1 handful fresh basil leaves

1 handful fresh parsley

5 to 6 sundried tomatoes

¼ cup/25 g finely grated parmesan

¼ cup/60 ml lemon juice

1 teaspoon salt

½ teaspoon pepper

½ teaspoon chili flakes

Pasta

1 pound/454 g dried pasta (linguini or spaghettini are both great choices)

Generous mound of grated parmesan for sprinkling

The great Popeye once said, "I'm strong to the finish 'cause I eats me spinach." Mind you, he also said, "Leave us not to jump to seclusions" and "Where is the entrance to the exit?" so take what you will from this.

TO MAKE THE SPINACH PESTO: Preheat the oven to 400°F/200°C. Use a piece of foil to make a little bowl, place the garlic inside, and drizzle with the olive oil. Pinch the top of the foil together to create a little pouch. Bake for 20 to 30 minutes, until the garlic is very soft and starting to caramelize around the edges. Remove from the oven and set aside to cool.

Lower the oven temperature to 350°F/180°C. Spread the walnuts across a baking sheet and bake until fragrant and toasted, 5 to 7 minutes. Make sure to give the pan a little toss at the halfway point for even toasting. Remove the oven and set aside to cool.

In the bowl of a food processor or blender, combine the two cloves of roasted and peeled garlic and the walnuts with the spinach, basil, parsley, sundried tomatoes, parmesan, lemon juice, salt, pepper, and chili flakes. Pulse to combine until mostly smooth, about 1 minute. Store the pesto sauce, covered, in the refrigerator for up to 1 week or in the freezer for up to 3 months.

TO MAKE THE PASTA: Fill a large pot with water and add a big tablespoon of salt. Bring the water to a rolling boil and add the dried pasta. Cook the pasta according to the package directions. When the pasta is done, drain the water off (reserve a small amount of pasta water in case you want to thin your pesto a smidge) and return the pot with the pasta to the stovetop. Add the pesto sauce and stir with a pair of tongs or spaghetti server to combine.

Spoon a big serving of pasta into each bowl and top with a small mountain of grated parmesan. *Buon appetito!*

TURKEY BURGER WITH RHUBARB KETCHUP

MAKES 4 BURGERS

1 cup/89 g panko breadcrumbs

¾ cup/180 ml water

1 pound/454 g ground turkey

⅓ cup/75 g butter, chilled and cut into ½-inch/1.25 cm cubes

1 tablespoon finely chopped fresh chives

1 tablespoon finely chopped fresh parsley

1 tablespoon finely chopped fresh basil

½ teaspoon chili flakes

2 teaspoons salt

½ teaspoon pepper

4 slices cheddar cheese (optional)

4 hamburger buns, split and lightly toasted and buttered

4 tablespoons mayonnaise

6 tablespoons Rhubarb Ketchup (page 134)

4 pieces butter lettuce, washed and dried

The secret to a great turkey burger is butter, soaked panko breadcrumbs, and rhubarb ketchup. Clearly, I'm no good at keeping secrets. But, hey, now that the cat is out of the bag, let's talk some more about how fabulous rhubarb ketchup is! Such a delicious alternative to Heinz and so much easier to get out of the damn bottle. Perfect slathered on a burger or simply spread on a good piece of bread topped with a thick slice of old cheddar. And yet another wonderful way to use up all that gorgeous rhubarb I hope you're growing in your garden (and fingers crossed some potatoes too, because a burger needs fries).

In a small bowl, combine the panko breadcrumbs and water and set aside for 5 to 10 minutes. Once the panko has softened and absorbed all the water, use your hands or the back of a large spoon to mash the panko to make a smooth paste.

Place the ground turkey in a large bowl and add the panko paste. Use your hands or a large spoon to blend them well.

Add the butter cubes, chives, parsley, basil, chili flakes, salt, and pepper and mix again to combine.

Divide the meat into four portions, shape into patties, and store in the refrigerator until you're ready to cook them.

You have a few options for cooking the patties. You can fire up the barbecue and grill them, or you can cook the patties in a frying pan over medium-high heat. (For the frying pan, there is no need to oil the pan, just get it nice and hot before you place the patties in it, making sure to leave a little space between each one.) Cook the burgers until they are nicely seared and the juices are starting to bubble up, about 5 minutes. Use a metal spatula to flip them over, top with cheddar cheese slices (if using), and continue to cook for another 3 to 5 minutes, until nicely seared on the outside and the juices run clear when poked. You can also bake the patties on a baking sheet in a preheated 350°F/180°C oven for 15 to 20 minutes; if you're baking the patties in the oven, top them with the cheese in the last couple of minutes of cook time.

Place both halves of the prepared hamburger buns, face side up, on a serving platter. Spread the bottom half with mayonnaise and the top half with the rhubarb ketchup. Place a burger patty on the bottom half of each bun and top with a piece of lettuce and the other half of the bun.

Continued

RHUBARB KETCHUP

MAKES ABOUT 2 CUPS/
500 ML

1 tablespoon olive oil

1 shallot, finely diced

1 pound/454 g fresh or frozen
  rhubarb stems, washed and
  cut into 1-inch/2.5 cm
  pieces

1 pound/454 g tomatoes,
  quartered with seeds
  removed

½ cup/100 g dark brown sugar

2 tablespoons apple cider
  vinegar

2 tablespoons red wine

1 teaspoon allspice

1 teaspoon salt

½ teaspoon pepper

In a large pot over medium-high heat, warm the olive oil. Add the diced shallot and cook until soft and just starting to brown, 3 to 4 minutes.

Add the rhubarb and tomatoes, using a wooden spoon to give everything a good stir to combine. Continue cooking until the rhubarb and tomatoes are starting to break down, 10 to 12 minutes.

Add the brown sugar, vinegar, wine, allspice, salt, and pepper and cook until everything has started to come together into a thick spread, another 5 to 8 minutes.

Remove from the heat and transfer to a bowl. Store, covered, in the refrigerator for up to 1 week.

SIDES

FRIED RADISHES IN BROWN BUTTER

MAKES 4 SERVINGS

2 bunches rainbow radishes
    with green tops, about
    1 pound/454 g

¼ cup/57 g Brown Butter
    (page 199)

1 teaspoon dark brown sugar

2 teaspoons finely chopped
    fresh rosemary

2 teaspoons fresh thyme leaves

1 teaspoon sea salt

Zest of 1 lemon

1 tablespoon fresh mint leaves,
    roughly torn

As odd as it may seem, radishes are just as delicious cooked as they are raw. Some would even say more so! Just like with people, it's important we don't pigeonhole our produce, or we'll never get to experience all they have to offer.

Remove the green tops from the radishes and rinse under cold water (or use a salad spinner) to clean them. Lay on paper towels and pat to dry.

Roughly tear the tops and set aside.

In a large heavy frying pan over medium-high heat, add the brown butter, radishes, brown sugar, rosemary, and thyme and continue to cook until the radishes start to char, 5 to 8 minutes.

Remove the pan from the heat and sprinkle with the sea salt and lemon zest.

Transfer the radishes to a serving bowl and use a large spoon to toss with the mint and reserved tops to serve.

RISOTTO WITH LEEKS, PEAS & SPINACH

MAKES 4 SERVINGS

5 cups/1.25 liters chicken stock

3 tablespoons butter

1 tablespoon olive oil

1 shallot, finely diced

1 leek, white and light green parts only, rinsed and thinly sliced crosswise

1 cup/225 g arborio rice

¼ cup/60 ml white wine

2 tablespoons lemon juice

1 teaspoon salt

½ teaspoon pepper

¾ cup/109 g fresh peas

1 big handful fresh spinach leaves, washed and mostly dried

1 cup/100 g grated parmesan

1 tablespoon fresh thyme leaves

1 tablespoon finely chopped fresh dill, plus a little more to serve

Zest of 1 lemon

A simple but elegant meal regardless of the season. This is delicious all on its own or makes a perfect side with grilled fish or meat.

Some lovely crusty bread, cold butter, and a bottle of Chablis wouldn't hurt either.

In a medium pot over high heat, bring the chicken stock to a boil. Remove from the heat and set aside.

In a large saucepan over medium heat, melt 2 tablespoons of the butter and the olive oil. Add the shallot and leek and sauté until translucent and tender. Add the rice and continue to sauté for several minutes until it too starts to appear slightly translucent. Add the wine, lemon juice, salt, and pepper and keep stirring until the rice has mostly absorbed the wine and juice.

Add a ladleful of the hot chicken stock and keep stirring until most of the stock has been absorbed, making sure to reduce the heat to a simmer so the stock doesn't boil away too quickly and cook only the outside of the rice. Add your next ladleful and repeat. Continue until all the stock has been absorbed. Have a taste and make sure the rice is cooked through. If you run out of stock before you feel the rice is done, you can add some boiling water. All in all, it should take 15 to 20 minutes to cook the rice.

Add the fresh peas, spinach, grated parmesan, thyme, dill, lemon zest, remaining 1 tablespoon of butter, and a little more salt and pepper to taste.

Spoon the risotto into shallow bowls and garnish with a sprig of dill to serve.

ROASTED CAULIFLOWER ON A BED OF ROMESCO

MAKES 4 TO 6 SERVINGS

1 small head cauliflower,
    cut into florets

1 tablespoon olive oil

1 teaspoon salt

½ teaspoon pepper

1 cup/250 ml Romesco Sauce
    (page 196)

1 tablespoon finely chopped
    parsley

1 tablespoon currants

1 tablespoon sliced almonds

My husband isn't a huge fan of cauliflower, but he does like romesco and currants. You see what I did there, right? Sometimes you have to fool the kids to get them to eat their vegetables.

Preheat the oven to 400°F/200°C. Line a baking sheet with parchment paper.

Spread the cauliflower florets across the baking sheet (I also like to include any of the tender leaves from the cauliflower if available), drizzle with the olive oil, and sprinkle with the salt and pepper. Use a large spoon or your hands to give it a toss and evenly coat in the oil.

Place the cauliflower on the center rack of the oven and bake until just starting to brown, 15 to 20 minutes. Use a spatula to give it all a toss at the halfway mark so that it roasts evenly.

Spread the prepared romesco across a platter or large plate and top with the roasted cauliflower.

Sprinkle the chopped parsley, currants, and sliced almonds over the cauliflower and serve.

ROASTED BRUSSELS SPROUTS WITH BALSAMIC & PARMESAN

MAKES 4 SERVINGS

2 pounds/900 g brussels
sprouts, washed and halved

2 tablespoons olive oil

1 tablespoon good balsamic
vinegar (the older and
more syrupy the better)

2 teaspoons sugar

1 teaspoon salt

1 teaspoon chili flakes

2 tablespoons butter

1 cup/100 g grated parmesan

Squeeze of lemon juice

Much like the rotary dial phone, advances in brussels sprout technology have been huge since the days of them being nothing more than a hideous side dish served at every holiday dinner. (Not to mention, their towering stalks create interest and drama in the garden!)

Preheat the oven to 400°F/200°C. Line a baking sheet with parchment paper.

Place the brussels sprouts on the baking sheet and drizzle with the olive oil. Sprinkle with the balsamic vinegar, sugar, salt, and chili flakes. Use a large spoon or your hands to combine and evenly coat everything.

Roast on the center rack of the oven for 20 to 25 minutes, until they are turning brown and getting crispy in parts.

Remove from the oven and add the butter and half of the parmesan. Use a large spoon or spatula to toss them all together.

Place the sprouts in a serving bowl, squeeze a wedge of lemon over them, and top with a mound of the remaining parmesan to serve.

POTATO FENNEL GRATIN

MAKES 4 SERVINGS

2 tablespoons butter

2 small leeks, white and
light green parts only,
finely chopped

2 pounds/900 g Yukon Gold
potatoes, thinly sliced

2 tablespoons fresh thyme
leaves

2 teaspoons salt

1 teaspoon pepper

1 small fennel bulb, thinly
sliced

1½ cups/165 g grated Gruyère

2 cups/500 ml whipping cream

As a child I wasn't a big fan of scalloped potatoes, but of course I hadn't written this recipe yet, so I can't blame me. I also had no idea how much better a potato tastes that has been freshly pulled from the garden. An education is a delicious thing.

Preheat the oven to 375°F/190°C. Butter an 8 × 8-inch/20 × 20 cm baking pan or casserole dish.

In a medium frying pan over medium heat, melt the butter and sauté the leeks until soft and just starting to brown, about 5 minutes.

Spoon a third of the leeks into the bottom of the buttered pan. Top with a third of the potato slices and season with a third of the thyme, salt, and pepper. Top with a third of the fennel slices and a third of the cheese. Repeat these steps two more times to create all the layers of the dish. Pour the cream around the edges of the pan, and then give the pan a gentle shake to help distribute the cream.

Bake for 40 to 45 minutes, until the cream is bubbling and the tip of a knife easily inserts into the potatoes. Remove from the oven and allow to cool slightly before serving so that it has a little time to firm up.

ROASTED BEETS WITH PINK GRAPEFRUIT

MAKES 4 TO 6 SERVINGS

3 large beets

Drizzle plus 2 tablespoons olive oil

Sprinkle plus ½ teaspoon salt

Sprinkle plus ½ teaspoon pepper

1 cup/250 ml plain yogurt

¼ cup/30 g crumbled feta cheese

Zest of 1 lemon

1 tablespoon white wine vinegar

1 large pink grapefruit, peeled and cut into segments

2 tablespoons roughly chopped pistachios

1 tablespoon fresh mint leaves, torn

This dish checks a lot of boxes . . . creamy, crunchy, juicy, and colorful! An easy-to-prepare feast for the eyes and stomach. I love it when my vegetables look as beautiful on the plate as they do in the garden!

Preheat the oven to 400°F/200°C. Rinse any dirt or debris off the beets and trim the tops and bottoms. Place the beets on a sheet of foil, drizzle with a little olive oil, and sprinkle with salt and pepper. Wrap them inside the foil and place directly on the oven rack to roast until fork tender, approximately 45 minutes.

Remove the beets from the oven and set aside until they are cool enough to handle. Remove the skin of the beets and cut each one into eight pieces.

In a small bowl, whisk together the yogurt, feta cheese, and lemon zest.

In another small bowl, whisk together the 2 tablespoons olive oil, the vinegar, and the ½ teaspoon each of salt and pepper.

On a medium-sized platter or large plate, spread the yogurt mixture.

Arrange the roasted beets and grapefruit segments across the yogurt. Sprinkle with pistachios, drizzle with the olive oil dressing, and finish with the torn mint leaves.

Best eaten straightaway, but if you have any left over you can mix it all up and keep it, covered, in the fridge for a couple of days.

PEAS & CRISPY PANCETTA

MAKES 4 TO 6 SERVINGS

2 thick slices pancetta, cut into little cubes

3 cups/435 g shelled fresh peas (you can also use frozen)

1 tablespoon butter

1 tablespoon lemon juice

1 tablespoon capers, roughly chopped

2 tablespoons finely chopped fresh mint

1 teaspoon salt

½ teaspoon pepper

1 or 2 slices mint Herb Butter (page 192), to serve

The only thing better than eating fresh peas straight from their shell would be frying them up with a little pancetta and lemon, which makes this recipe VERY convenient.

In a large frying pan over medium-high heat, cook the pancetta for several minutes until it starts to get brown and crispy, 8 to 10 minutes.

Lower the heat to medium and add the peas, butter, lemon juice, and capers. Cook just until the peas turn a lovely bright green, 5 to 7 minutes. If you overcook them, the color won't be as pretty, but they'll still be delicious.

Remove the pan from the heat and stir in the chopped mint, salt, and pepper. Transfer the hot peas to a serving dish and top with a slice or two of the mint butter to serve.

FLUFFY STUFFED POTATOES

MAKES 4 TO 8 SERVINGS

4 large russet potatoes, washed

1 tablespoon finely chopped fresh dill

1 tablespoon finely chopped fresh parsley, plus a little extra for garnish

1 tablespoon finely chopped fresh chives

½ cup/55 g grated cheddar cheese

¼ cup/43 g crumbled goat cheese

½ cup/125 ml whipping cream

2 large eggs, separated

2 tablespoons butter, plus a little extra for garnish

1½ teaspoons salt

1 teaspoon pepper

A very convenient and delicious way to serve mashed potatoes without the need of a serving bowl or spoon! You can prepare the potatoes up to the point of their final bake earlier in the day or even the night before and then finish them off just prior to serving.

Preheat the oven to 400°F/200°C. Line a baking sheet with parchment paper.

Use a fork to pierce each potato three to four times. Place the potatoes directly on the center rack in the oven and bake for 50 to 60 minutes, until fork tender.

Remove the potatoes from the oven and allow to cool slightly before slicing each one in half lengthwise. Use a large spoon to scoop out the insides of the cooked potatoes and place them in a large bowl. If you have a food mill or tamis (very fine–mesh sieve) you can run the inside of the potatoes through it to ensure they are smooth (but it's not entirely necessary, as a few little lumps won't hurt).

Place the empty skins on the prepared baking sheet and set aside.

Add the fresh herbs, cheddar and goat cheese, cream, egg yolks, butter, salt, and pepper to the bowl with the potato flesh and use a wooden spoon to stir to combine. Have a taste and adjust seasoning as needed. I find potatoes benefit from a heavier hand with salt but you're the best judge.

In a stand mixer fitted with the whisk attachment, beat the egg whites until stiff. Use a rubber spatula to gently fold the egg whites into the potato mixture.

Fill each potato skin with an equal amount of potato filling and bake for 15 to 20 minutes, until the tops are starting to lightly brown.

Remove the potatoes from the oven and top with a little pat of butter and a sprinkle of chopped parsley.

ROASTED CARROTS WITH CARROT TOP PESTO

MAKES 4 SERVINGS

Carrots

10 to 12 medium-sized carrots (about 2 pounds/900 g), washed and peeled, green tops reserved for the pesto

2 tablespoons olive oil, plus more for drizzling

1 teaspoon salt, plus more for sprinkling

1 teaspoon pepper

1 teaspoon sugar

Carrot Top Pesto

1 big handful walnuts

2 handfuls carrot top greens, plus a little extra for sprinkling

1 handful fresh mint leaves

½ cup/50 g grated parmesan

¼ cup/60 ml lemon juice

1 teaspoon salt

½ teaspoon pepper

Sort of a nose-to-tail recipe if carrots had noses and tails.

TO MAKE THE CARROTS: Preheat the oven to 400°F/200°C. Line a baking sheet with parchment paper.

Spread the carrots across the baking sheet. Drizzle with the olive oil and sprinkle with the salt, pepper, and sugar. Use your hands to roll the carrots around in the oil and seasoning to help coat them.

Bake for 20 to 25 minutes, giving the pan a few shakes at the halfway point to help the carrots brown evenly, until the carrots are just fork tender.

TO MAKE THE PESTO: In a blender or the bowl of a food processor, combine the pesto ingredients and blend on high until just combined but not smooth.

Spread the pesto across a serving platter and top with the baked carrots. Drizzle a little olive oil over the carrots and sprinkle with the reserved carrot top greens and a smidge more salt to serve.

CREAMY, CHEESY KALE BAKE

MAKES 4 TO 6 SERVINGS

Kale

2 tablespoons butter

1 tablespoon olive oil

1 large onion, finely diced

2 bunches kale, washed,
    spines removed, and
    roughly chopped

1 teaspoon salt

½ teaspoon pepper

2 tablespoons all-purpose flour

1 cup/250 ml whipping cream

¼ cup/25 g grated parmesan

1 cup/115 g grated cheddar
    cheese

1 teaspoon chili flakes

Topping

1 tablespoon butter

1 cup/90 g panko breadcrumbs

1 teaspoon finely chopped
    fresh parsley

½ teaspoon salt

½ teaspoon pepper

I've discovered that the easiest way to convert someone into a lover of kale is through a heavy smothering of cream and cheese and a sprinkle of buttery breadcrumbs. To clarify, these additions are to enhance the kale, not to torture your reluctant dinner guest.

Preheat the oven to 350°F/180°C. Lightly butter an 8 × 8-inch/20 × 20 cm pan.

TO MAKE THE KALE: In a large frying pan over medium-high heat, melt the butter and olive oil. Add the onion and cook until it is soft and translucent, 5 to 7 minutes.

Add the chopped kale and continue to cook, stirring with a wooden spoon or spatula, until it has fully softened and just started to brown, 5 to 7 minutes. Add the salt and pepper and stir again.

Sprinkle the flour across the kale and stir again to combine. Add the cream, parmesan, cheddar, and chili flakes and continue to cook until the cheese has melted and the cream is just starting to boil. Transfer the kale mixture to the prepared pan and use the back of the spoon or spatula to smooth it over.

TO MAKE THE TOPPING: In a small frying pan over medium-high heat, melt the butter. Add the breadcrumbs, parsley, salt, and pepper. Use a wooden spoon or spatula to stir until the breadcrumbs are fully coated in butter and then spread them across the kale.

Bake until the cheesy cream has begun to bubble up and the breadcrumbs are a lovely golden brown, 20 to 25 minutes.

SWEETS

ROASTED BALSAMIC STRAWBERRY SHORTCAKES

MAKES 6 SERVINGS

Roasted Balsamic Strawberries

2 pounds/900 g strawberries, washed and dried

¼ cup/50 g sugar

2 tablespoons balsamic vinegar

1 teaspoon vanilla paste

¼ teaspoon salt

Whipped Cream

2 cups/500 ml whipping cream

¼ cup/30 g icing sugar

1 teaspoon vanilla paste

6 Graham Scones (page 166)

A fresh strawberry is a delicious thing and maybe even a little more so if picked from your very own patch. Roasting the strawberries will further enhance their sweetness, which balances nicely with the tartness of the balsamic. Mind you, a pile of whipped cream and a scone doesn't hurt either.

TO MAKE THE ROASTED BALSAMIC STRAWBERRIES: Preheat the oven to 400°F/200°C. Line a baking sheet with parchment paper.

Use a small paring knife to remove the leaf caps from all the strawberries and place the strawberries in a large mixing bowl (the strawberries will shrink down when they roast, so there is no need to cut them).

Add the sugar, balsamic vinegar, vanilla paste, and salt to the bowl with the strawberries and use a large spoon to gently toss them to coat.

Spread the strawberries across the prepared baking sheet. Roast in the oven for 20 to 25 minutes until they have softened and the sugar has started to caramelize. Remove from the oven and set aside to cool.

TO MAKE THE WHIPPED CREAM: In a stand mixer fitted with the whisk attachment, combine the cream, icing sugar, and vanilla paste and beat on high until soft peaks form.

To serve, place each scone on a serving plate and split in half. Spoon a big dollop of whipped cream on the bottom half of each scone and top with a generous serving of the roasted strawberries. Place the remaining scone half back on top of each one and serve.

NOTE: *The roasted strawberries are just as wonderful served over a bowl of ice cream or your morning bowl of oatmeal.*

Continued

GRAHAM SCONES

MAKES EIGHT 3-INCH/
7.5 CM SCONES

3 cups/360 g all-purpose flour

1 cup/100 g graham crumbs,
    plus a little more for
    sprinkling

¾ cup/150 g sugar

2 tablespoons baking powder

½ teaspoon salt

1 cup/227 g butter, chilled
    and cut into 1-inch/2.5 cm
    cubes

1 cup/250 ml buttermilk

1 egg, lightly beaten

Coarse sanding sugar,
    for sprinkling

Preheat the oven to 400°F/200°C. Line a baking sheet with parchment paper.

In a stand mixer fitted with a paddle attachment, quickly mix the flour, graham crumbs, sugar, baking powder, and salt on low speed to blend. Add the butter cubes and mix until large crumbs form.

Add the buttermilk to the bowl and beat again until almost combined.

Turn the dough out onto a lightly floured work surface and roll out to about 1 inch/2.5 cm thick. Use a 3-inch/7.5 cm circular cutter to cut out eight circles and place them on the prepared baking sheet about 1½ inches/ 3.75 cm apart.

Use a pastry brush to gently coat the top of each scone with the beaten egg and sprinkle them with a little bit of graham crumbs and the coarse sanding sugar.

Bake for approximately 20 minutes, until golden brown and a wood skewer inserted into the center comes out clean. Remove from the oven and serve warm with jam and butter or allow them to cool slightly before filling with whipped cream and roasted balsamic strawberries (page 165).

NOTE: *I made these scones to fill with roasted strawberries and cream for a delicious summer dessert, but I soon discovered they are also stupendous at breakfast, lightly toasted with butter and jam.*

FLORAL SHORTBREAD COINS

MAKES 18 COOKIES

1 cup/227 g butter, room
temperature

½ cup/100 g sugar, plus more
for sprinkling

2 teaspoons vanilla paste

2 cups/240 g all-purpose flour

Selection of fresh edible
flowers or herbs

*In an ode to Lori Stern, a true culinary artist . . . I can't imagine a more
delicious bouquet. I chose one of my favorite flowers for these cookies, pansies,
but your garden has so much more to offer. Nasturtium, calendula, chamomile,
roses, or lavender would be beautiful choices too! But remember, not all flowers
are edible, so do research your choice if you are unsure.*

Preheat the oven to 350°F/180°C. Line a baking sheet with parchment
paper.

In a stand mixer fitted with a paddle attachment, cream the butter, sugar,
and vanilla paste on medium to high speed until light and fluffy. Scrape
down the sides of the bowl.

Turn the mixer to low, add the flour, and mix until fully combined.

Place the dough on a lightly floured work surface. Using a rolling pin, roll
out the dough to ½ inch/1.25 cm thick. Use a 2-inch/5 cm circular cutter
to cut out eighteen circles. Transfer to the prepared baking sheet and place
about ½ inch/1.25 cm apart.

Bake for 12 to 15 minutes or until the cookies are lightly golden brown
around the edges.

Remove the cookies from the oven and carefully press a pansy, rose petal, or
edible flower of your choice onto the top of each cookie. Hold the petal or
flower down for a few seconds until the heat of the cookie has made it stick.
Repeat with the remaining cookies and then sprinkle with sugar to finish.
Transfer to a wire rack to cool.

COCONUT CREAM PAVLOVA

MAKES ONE 9-INCH/23 CM
PAVLOVA, 6 TO 8 SERVINGS

Pavlova

1 cup/100 g large-flake
  unsweetened coconut

5 egg whites

½ teaspoon cream of tartar

1½ cups/300 g sugar

1 teaspoon coconut flavoring

1 teaspoon white vinegar

¼ cup/28 g unsweetened
  medium shredded coconut

Coconut Cream

1 cup/250 ml whipping cream

¼ cup/30 g icing sugar

1 teaspoon vanilla paste

1 recipe Coconut Curd
  (page 172)

If coconut cream pie and pavlova had a baby . . . so good you'll wish they had twins! A big thank you to my three lovely ladies, Coco, Regina, and Olive, for happily providing the delicious eggs for this recipe.

TO MAKE THE PAVLOVA: Preheat the oven to 350°F/180°C. Line a deep 9-inch/23 cm cake pan or springform pan with parchment paper. This is best achieved by laying one piece of parchment across another piece in a "t" shape. Press the two crossed sheets into the pan, making little folds in the sides as necessary to get the paper to create a circular shape. Allow the excess paper to simply hang over the sides of the pan.

Spread the flaked coconut across a small baking sheet or pan. Bake for 3 to 5 minutes, until the coconut is toasted and beginning to turn a lovely golden brown. Remove from the oven and set aside to cool.

In a stand mixer fitted with the whisk attachment, beat the egg whites on high speed until foamy. Add the cream of tartar and continue to beat until soft peaks form. Make sure your mixer bowl and whisk attachment are free of any traces of fat, as even the tiniest amount will prevent your egg whites from whisking properly.

Turn the mixer speed to medium-low and slowly start to add the sugar, 1 tablespoon at a time. Once all the sugar has been added, turn the mixer to medium-high and continue to beat until your egg whites form stiff peaks, 5 to 8 minutes. Turn the mixer down and add the coconut flavoring and vinegar.

Beat again, then add the shredded coconut and beat just until combined. Make sure not to overbeat your meringue. It is done when the meringue reaches soft peaks: pull the beater from the bowl and hold it upright; the peak of the meringue should hold with just the top folding over.

Use a rubber spatula to transfer the meringue to the prepared pan and then gently push it into place and roughly smooth the top over.

Continued

Bake for 40 to 45 minutes. The outside of the pavlova should be pale and crisp, with the inside being slightly soft and a bit sticky when a wooden skewer is inserted in the middle. Don't worry if the center of the pavlova falls; that's where all the lovely coconut cream will go!

Allow the pavlova to cool before lifting it by the edges of parchment paper to remove it from the pan.

TO MAKE THE COCONUT CREAM: In a stand mixer fitted with the whisk attachment, beat the cream, icing sugar, and vanilla paste on high until soft peaks form.

Gently fold the whipped cream into the bowl of coconut curd in three additions until combined.

Spoon the coconut cream into the center of the pavlova and top with the toasted coconut flakes.

COCONUT CURD

MAKES 1 CUP/250 ML

1 cup/250 ml coconut milk

3 egg yolks

½ cup/100 g sugar

3 tablespoons all-purpose flour

1 tablespoon butter

½ teaspoon vanilla paste

In a small pot over medium heat, whisk together the coconut milk, egg yolks, and sugar. Sprinkle the flour across the top and whisk to combine. Turn the heat to medium-high and continue to whisk until the mixture becomes thick like pudding, about 5 minutes.

Remove the pot from the heat and stir in the butter and vanilla paste.

Strain the curd through a fine sieve into a bowl, cover with plastic wrap, and place in the refrigerator to cool.

This curd will keep in an airtight container in the refrigerator for up to 1 week.

NOTE: *I am a big fan of coconut. If you're not or you just want to change things up a little, you can always use whole milk instead of the coconut milk to make a vanilla pastry cream.*

LEMON THYME CHIFFON CAKE

MAKES ONE 9-INCH/23 CM
CAKE, 8 TO 10 SERVINGS

Chiffon Cake

2 cups/210 g pastry flour

1 tablespoon baking powder

½ teaspoon salt

1½ cups/300 g sugar

8 large eggs, separated

½ cup/125 ml vegetable oil

½ cup/125 ml water

¼ cup/60 ml lemon juice

Zest of 1 lemon

2 teaspoons vanilla

1 tablespoon fresh thyme leaves

½ teaspoon cream of tartar

Glaze

1½ cups/180 g icing sugar

4 to 5 tablespoons/60 to 75 ml
 lemon juice

I've read that thyme has medicinal qualities, so I'm sure a couple of slices of this cake will cure all that ails you. If you aren't growing thyme in your garden, not to worry. You can omit it and just make a lovely lemon chiffon cake.

TO MAKE THE CHIFFON CAKE: Preheat the oven to 350°F/180°C. On a large piece of parchment paper, sift the flour, baking powder, and salt. Set aside.

In a large mixing bowl, whisk together 1 cup/200 g of the sugar with the egg yolks, oil, water, lemon juice, lemon zest, and vanilla. Add the sifted dry ingredients and fresh thyme and whisk to combine.

In a stand mixer fitted with the whisk attachment, beat the egg whites on high until foamy. Add the cream of tartar and continue beating until stiff peaks form.

Turn the mixer to medium and slowly beat in the remaining ½ cup/100 g of sugar a few tablespoons at a time. Turn the mixer to high speed and continue to beat until the egg whites are smooth and glossy, 3 to 5 minutes more.

Using a rubber spatula, gently fold the egg whites into the cake batter in three even additions.

Transfer the batter to a 9-inch/23 cm angel food/tube pan and use the spatula to spread it evenly around the pan.

Bake for approximately 40 to 45 minutes or until a wooden skewer inserted in the center of the cake comes out clean.

Remove the cake from the oven and invert the pan to cool. If your tube pan doesn't have little feet to support it when inverted, you can always set it atop a wine bottle neck. Allow the cake to cool completely before removing it from the pan and flipping it right side up.

TO MAKE THE GLAZE: In a small bowl, combine the icing sugar and enough of the lemon juice to make a thin glaze. Place the cooled cake on the serving plate or cake stand and spoon the glaze over the top, allowing it to drip down the sides.

CHOCOLATE ZUCCHINI CAKE WITH CREAM CHEESE WHIP

Zucchini Cake

1¾ cups/185 g pastry flour

¼ cup/18 g cocoa powder

1 teaspoon baking soda

½ teaspoon baking powder

½ teaspoon salt

1 cup/250 ml vegetable oil

1 cup/200 g sugar

2 large eggs

1 tablespoon vanilla

1 tablespoon instant espresso
   powder

½ cup/125 ml hot water

1½ cups/185 g grated zucchini

Cream Cheese Whip

1 cup/227 g cold cream cheese
   (the real deal, not the
   spreadable kind) (see Note)

½ cup/60 g icing sugar

1 cup/250 ml cold whipping
   cream (see Note)

1 teaspoon vanilla paste
   (see Note)

This is an easy one-bowl cake that comes together in a flash. To make it even easier, I chose to bake it in a deep springform pan so there is no fussing or mussing with cake layers and icing. However, I encourage you to put an extra-generous pile of icing on the top of the cake so no one feels shortchanged in that department. This cream cheese whip recipe has become one of my personal favorites—it's a much lighter alternative to the buttercream I have traditionally iced my cakes with but honestly just as delicious!

TO MAKE THE ZUCCHINI CAKE: Position the rack in the center of the oven and preheat to 350°F/180°C. Butter and flour a deep 8-inch/20 cm cake pan or a springform pan. (If you would prefer to make a layer cake, you can also use two regular 8-inch/20 cm cake pans and divide the batter evenly between them.)

On a large piece of parchment paper, sift the flour, cocoa, baking soda, baking powder, and salt. Set aside.

In a large mixing bowl, whisk together the vegetable oil and sugar. Add the eggs and vanilla and continue to whisk until well combined.

In a small bowl, combine the espresso powder and hot water and stir to dissolve. Add the coffee to the batter and whisk to combine.

Sprinkle the dry ingredients over the batter and whisk again to combine. Add the grated zucchini to the batter and use a rubber spatula or wooden spoon to combine.

Place the batter in the prepared pan. Bake for 45 to 50 minutes or until a wooden skewer inserted into the center comes out clean.

TO MAKE THE CREAM CHEESE WHIP: In a stand mixer fitted with the paddle attachment, beat the cream cheese on high speed until very soft. Scrape down the sides of the bowl with a rubber spatula. Turn the mixer to low and add the icing sugar. Continue to beat on low until well combined. Scrape down the sides of the bowl again.

With the mixer still running on low, slowly add the cream. Once incorporated, turn the mixer to high and continue to beat until light and fluffy. Add the vanilla paste and beat again to combine.

Continued

Remove the cake from the oven and allow to cool for about 10 minutes. Invert the cake onto a wire rack to cool completely.

Transfer the cake to a serving plate or cake stand and generously spread the cream cheese whip across the top.

NOTE: *Very important to the success of this cream cheese whip recipe is the temperature of your ingredients: make sure your cream cheese and cream are nice and cold! If not, the fat will not be able to emulsify, meaning it won't be able to hold air particles, which will prevent those lovely soft peaks from forming. If you don't have vanilla paste, you can always substitute 2 teaspoons of vanilla extract or the inside of one vanilla pod.*

MIXED BERRY BUCKWHEAT LOAF

MAKES ONE 8-INCH/20 CM
LOAF

1½ cups/180 g all-purpose flour

½ cup/60 g buckwheat flour

¾ teaspoon baking powder

½ teaspoon baking soda

¾ teaspoon salt

¾ cup/170 g butter, melted

1 cup/200 g sugar

3 large eggs

¾ cup/180 ml buttermilk

1 teaspoon vanilla

1 cup/170 g mixed fresh berries
  (raspberries, blueberries,
  blackberries . . . your call)

1 tablespoon icing sugar

I have developed a real love for buckwheat! On top of the delicious nutty flavor it imparts, it's also considered by many in the nutritional field to be one of the healthiest grains available. So please feel free to have several slices.

Preheat the oven to 350°F/180°C. Butter and flour an 8-inch/20 cm loaf pan. On a large piece of parchment paper, sift the all-purpose flour, buckwheat flour, baking powder, baking soda, and salt.

In a large mixing bowl, whisk the melted butter and sugar to combine. Add the eggs, whisking well after each addition. Add the buttermilk and vanilla and whisk again.

Add the dry ingredients and whisk again to combine.

Use a rubber spatula to gently fold in the mixed berries to avoid crushing them (you could also make this recipe with frozen berries and save yourself the worry).

Place the batter in the prepared pan. Bake for 50 to 60 minutes or until a wooden skewer inserted in the center comes out clean. Remove from the oven and allow to cool for about 10 minutes before removing the loaf from the pan and transferring to a wire rack to cool completely. Gently sift a light dusting of icing sugar across the top of the loaf.

Store, covered, for up to 1 week or in the freezer for up to 3 months.

RHUBARB PANNA COTTA

MAKES 6 SERVINGS

Rhubarb

2 cups/200 g chopped rhubarb
  stems

2 tablespoons sugar

1 teaspoon lemon juice

Panna Cotta

1 envelope/2.5 teaspoons/7 g
  unflavored gelatin

¼ cup/60 ml water

3 cups/750 ml whipping cream

½ cup/100 g sugar

1½ teaspoons vanilla paste

½ teaspoon salt

Graham Topping

¼ cup/25 g graham crumbs

1 tablespoon sugar

This recipe is all about textures: silky panna cotta, chunky jammy rhubarb, and the slight crunch of the sugary graham crumbs make every mouthful perfect. If you aren't a fan of the rhubarb or graham, you can simply omit them as the panna cotta is just as lovely topped with fresh berries.

Place six glass compotes (ideally ¾ cup/180 ml size) or ramekins (see Note) on a small baking sheet or tray and set aside.

TO MAKE THE RHUBARB: In a small saucepan, combine the rhubarb, sugar, and lemon juice over medium-high heat and stir to combine. Continue to stir for another 5 to 8 minutes, until the sugar starts to melt. Reduce the heat to medium and continue to cook until the rhubarb has broken down and become quite mushy, like a chunky jam.

Divide the rhubarb evenly between the six compotes and set aside.

TO MAKE THE PANNA COTTA: In a small saucepan, warm the gelatin and water over medium heat until the gelatin has dissolved. Remove from the heat.

In another saucepan over medium heat, whisk together the cream, sugar, vanilla paste, and salt. Adjust the heat to bring it to a boil. Remove the pan from the heat and whisk in the gelatin mixture until combined.

Divide the panna cotta mixture among the compotes, carefully pouring it atop the rhubarb in each one. Place the panna cotta tray in the refrigerator until they just start to set, about 1 hour.

TO MAKE THE GRAHAM TOPPING: In a small bowl, stir to combine the graham crumbs and sugar.

Remove the tray of compotes from the refrigerator and sprinkle the top of each one with approximately ¾ tablespoon of graham crumbs. Return the tray to the refrigerator until the panna cotta has fully set, at least 3 hours or overnight.

NOTE: *If you have chosen to use ramekins, you will need to release each panna cotta onto a plate to fully appreciate the layers when serving. To do this, simply set the ramekins in a shallow bowl of hot water for a few seconds, making sure the water only rises halfway up the side of the ramekin.*

Run a small knife around the edge of the panna cotta and then invert it over a small dessert plate. Gently lift the ramekin to release it.

RHUBARB BANANA BREAD WITH CRUMBLE

MAKES ONE 8-INCH/20 CM LOAF

Crumble

⅓ cup/40 g all-purpose flour

¼ teaspoon cinnamon

2 tablespoons light brown sugar

2 tablespoons butter

Pinch of salt

Rhubarb Banana Bread

1¾ cups/210 g all-purpose flour

½ teaspoon baking soda

1 teaspoon baking powder

½ teaspoon salt

¾ cup/170 g butter, room temperature

1 cup/200 g tightly packed light brown sugar

2 large eggs

2 bananas, mashed

½ cup/125 ml plain yogurt

1 teaspoon vanilla

1½ cups/150 g rhubarb stems, washed and cut into 1-inch/2.5 cm pieces

Can there ever be enough banana bread recipes in this world? I think not, and here's hoping that once you try this one you will agree. The lovely crumble topping and tart rhubarb chunks are pretty hard to argue with.

TO MAKE THE CRUMBLE: In a small bowl, use a fork (or your hands) to combine the ingredients for the crumble topping until large buttery crumbs form. Set aside.

TO MAKE THE RHUBARB BANANA BREAD: Preheat the oven to 350°F/180°C. Butter and flour an 8-inch/20 cm loaf pan. On a large piece of parchment paper, sift together the flour, baking soda, baking powder, and salt.

In a stand mixer fitted with the paddle attachment, cream the butter and sugar on medium-high speed until light and fluffy. Scrape down the sides of the bowl.

Add the eggs one at a time, and beat well after each addition. Scrape down the sides of the bowl again. Add the mashed bananas, yogurt, and vanilla and beat again.

Turn the mixer to low and slowly add the dry ingredients until just combined.

Add the rhubarb pieces and beat again to combine.

Pour the batter into the prepared pan. Use a spatula to lightly smooth over the top, and sprinkle with the crumble topping.

Bake for approximately 1 hour or until a wooden skewer inserted in the middle comes out clean.

Remove the loaf from the oven and allow it to cool slightly, then transfer to a wire rack to cool completely. This loaf will keep, covered, for up to 1 week or in the freezer for up to 3 months.

PANTRY STAPLES

HERB SALT

MAKES ABOUT ¾ CUP/225 G

3 handfuls mixed herbs (any
combination of basil,
rosemary, thyme, oregano,
parsley, mint, etc.), leaves
only

1 lemon rind, all pith removed

½ cup/150 g kosher salt

*More Mrs. Daykin than Mrs. Dash, this salt is wonderful sprinkled on
fish, meat, roast vegetables, simple salad greens, corn on the cob, or even
poached eggs.*

Preheat the oven to 325°F/160°C. Line a baking sheet with parchment
paper.

Spread the fresh herb mixture and lemon rind across the prepared baking
sheet. Bake until everything feels dry to the touch, 20 to 25 minutes, using
a large spoon or spatula to turn the herbs every 5 minutes to make sure
nothing is browning.

Remove from the oven and allow the herbs to cool completely before
transferring them to a blender or the bowl of a food processor. Add the
salt and blend on high until the herbs are very fine.

Store the herb salt in an airtight container or jar for up to 1 year.

HERB BUTTER

MAKES 2 SMALL ROLLS OF
BUTTER (I CUP/227 G)

1 cup/227 g salted butter, room
temperature (see Note)

2 large handfuls fresh herbs,
finely chopped (see Note)

1 teaspoon of lemon zest

I've always got a roll or two of herb butter in my freezer. There are no hard and fast rules when making this recipe, so have some fun with it. Different combinations of herbs, spices, or seasonings are yours to choose, but I have given you a few suggestions to get you started (see the Note below). This herb butter is perfect on a piece of grilled fish or meat, or you can finish your mashed potatoes or vegetables with a few slices of it (see the recipe for Peas & Crispy Pancetta on page 153), or just spread some inside a hamburger bun or sandwich!

Place all the ingredients in a stand mixer fitted with a paddle attachment and beat on high until well combined.

Place a piece of plastic wrap on the kitchen counter, then transfer half the butter mixture on top of the wrap. Shape the butter into a log about 4 inches/10 cm long and 2 inches/5 cm across, then wrap the plastic wrap tightly around it. Repeat with the remaining butter.

Place the logs in the refrigerator and allow to chill until firm, 25 to 30 minutes, before slicing.

NOTE: *I have chosen to use salted butter, but if you only have unsalted butter on hand, make sure to add ½ teaspoon of salt when blending.*

Some flavor combination ideas: Try dill and lemon, lovely on grilled halibut or salmon; add 1 clove minced garlic plus rosemary and oregano, and your lamb chops or roast potatoes will thank you; or chives and 1 tablespoon horseradish is the perfect combination to top a steak right off the grill; and mint and parsley are peas' best friend!

ROASTED TOMATO SAUCE

MAKES ABOUT 4 CUPS/
1 LITER

4 pounds/1.8 kg tomatoes cut in half (Roma tomatoes are a good choice but any combo of tomatoes will work. Just try to keep the size as uniform as possible so they roast evenly.)

1 small onion, peeled and quartered

2 cloves garlic, peeled

2 tablespoons olive oil

2 teaspoons balsamic vinegar

1 tablespoon Italian seasoning

1½ teaspoons salt

1 teaspoon pepper

My freezer runneth over with tomato sauce, and I wouldn't have it any other way. If you have a container of this tomato sauce on hand, you will always be able to make a meal. From a humble bowl of pasta to a pizza, the base for a simple soup, or my Vegetable Cannelloni (page 123), I promise it will save you every time.

Preheat the oven to 425°F/220°C.

Line two baking sheets with parchment paper and divide the tomatoes, onion, and garlic evenly between them.

Drizzle both sheets with the olive oil and balsamic vinegar and then evenly sprinkle with the Italian seasoning and salt and pepper.

Bake until fully roasted and starting to char, about 30 minutes.

Remove the trays from the oven and allow them to cool slightly before blending. Remove the roasted onion from both trays and discard.

Use a ricer to blend the roasted tomatoes and garlic into a large mixing bowl. If you don't own a ricer, you can use a food processor or blender, but don't overdo it. I like there to still be lots of texture to the sauce.

The tomato sauce will keep, covered, in the fridge for up to 1 week or in the freezer for up to 3 months.

ROMESCO SAUCE

MAKES ABOUT 2 CUPS/
500 ML

1 large red pepper

2 cloves garlic

¾ cup/105 g almonds

4 medium tomatoes, halved
  and seeds removed

1 big handful parsley leaves,
  roughly chopped

⅓ cup/80 ml olive oil

2 teaspoons lemon juice

1 tablespoon red wine vinegar

2 teaspoons sugar

1 teaspoon smoked paprika

½ teaspoon cayenne

1 teaspoon lemon zest

1 teaspoon salt

½ teaspoon pepper

An easy sauce to whip up when you want to add just a smidge more flavor to a dish. This recipe works wonders atop a piece of grilled fish, spread inside a chicken sandwich or burger, or, of course, as a delicious bed for roasted cauliflower (page 144). If you're in a terrible rush, you can always purchase a jar of roasted peppers at the grocery store and skip the roasting pepper step, but then you can't brag about the delicious pepper you grew (or you can, and I won't say a word).

Preheat the oven to broil on high. Line a baking sheet with foil. Place the rack just above the center point of the oven as you don't want the baking sheet too close to the broiler, which could char the pepper before it is actually roasted through.

Lay the pepper on its side on the prepared baking sheet and place under the broiler. Use tongs to turn the pepper every 5 minutes or so until it is roasted and charred, about 15 minutes. Remove the roasted pepper from the oven, place it in a paper bag, and fold over the top to close it. Allow the pepper to steam for about 15 minutes.

Meanwhile, preheat the oven to 350°F/180°C. Place the peeled garlic cloves on a small piece of foil and drizzle with a little olive oil. Pinch the foil closed to create a little package. Roast in the oven for about 20 minutes, until the garlic has softened and started to color. Allow to cool.

Remove the pepper from the bag and use a small knife to scrape away the skin; now that it has steamed, the skin should come away very easily. Slice the pepper open, remove and discard the stem and the remaining seeds, and roughly chop. Transfer to a large serving bowl.

Lower the oven temperature to 325°F/160°C. Place the almonds on a baking sheet or in a small baking pan and roast in the oven until evenly browned and fragrant, about 10 minutes. Give the pan a shake a couple of times throughout cooking to ensure even roasting.

In a blender or food processor, blend the roasted almonds on high until finely ground. Add the rest of the ingredients and blend again until nearly smooth.

Romesco sauce will keep, covered, in the fridge for up to 1 week or in the freezer for up to 3 months.

OLIVE TAPENADE

MAKES ABOUT 2 CUPS/
500 ML

2 cloves garlic

1 can (14 fl oz/398 ml/396 g)
    pitted green olives, drained

1 can (14 fl oz/398 ml/396 g)
    pitted black olives, drained

1 tablespoon capers

1 handful fresh parsley leaves,
    roughly chopped

1 handful fresh oregano leaves,
    roughly chopped

1 handful fresh basil leaves,
    roughly chopped

2 tablespoons lemon juice

Zest of 1 lemon

1 tablespoon balsamic vinegar

½ cup/125 ml olive oil

A good tapenade, like this one, can be a real workhorse in the kitchen. I created this recipe to layer into my Tomato Galette (page 125), but it works just as well as a dip with flatbread (page 59) or spread some across toasted baguette slices topped with shaved parmesan and basil for an easy appetizer. You could even add a dollop to the Red Pepper Bisque (page 102) in lieu of the crab for a vegetarian alternative.

Preheat the oven to 350°F/180°C. Place the peeled garlic cloves on a small piece of foil and drizzle with a little olive oil. Pinch the foil closed to create a little package. Roast in the oven for about 20 minutes, until the garlic has softened and started to color. Allow to cool.

In the bowl of a food processor fitted with the blade attachment, combine the olives, capers, roasted garlic, herbs, lemon juice, lemon zest, and balsamic vinegar and pulse to combine.

With the food processor running, slowly add the olive oil and blend until a chunky paste forms. You may need to scrape down the sides of the bowl a couple of times in the process to ensure it is evenly blended. Season with a little salt and pepper if you feel it needs it, but I find the olives provide enough for my taste.

The tapenade will keep, covered, in the refrigerator for 5 to 7 days.

BROWN BUTTER

MAKES 1 POUND/454 G

1 pound/454 g salted or
unsalted butter

This isn't so much a recipe as it is a method, but it is a necessary one at that. Brown butter is a staple in my kitchen; I like to prepare a batch and keep it in the freezer so I always have it on hand. By simply cooking the butter past the melting point, the milk solids will separate and toast, giving the butter a wonderful nutty and caramelized flavor. It works beautifully in lieu of regular butter in sauces for pasta, when pan-frying fish, or when baking cookies or cakes.

In a large, heavy-bottomed saucepan, melt the butter over medium heat. Use a light-colored or stainless-steel pan so that you can see the butter clearly as it browns. As it melts, use a spatula to swirl the butter in the pan. The butter will foam and sizzle. Continue to stir, and don't get distracted or walk away as it takes only a moment to go from deliciously browned to burned!

After 8 to 10 minutes, the foam will begin to subside, and you'll see lovely little brown bits forming at the bottom of the pan. Remove the pan from the heat and pour the butter into a bowl to stop the cooking.

Once it has cooled slightly, transfer it to a sheet pan lined with plastic wrap and place it in the freezer. Once the butter is frozen solid, lift it from the pan, remove the plastic wrap liner, and cut it into small squares. Place the frozen squares in an airtight container and store in the freezer for several months to use as needed.

THE CHICKENS

CHICKENS 101

I debated where to start when discussing the pros and cons of chicken ownership, but ultimately decided it was best to break the ice with brutal honesty. I believe that chickens, like any other pet, add a richness and quality to your life. My vegetables and flowers are truly beautiful, but in the absence of my ladies, I worry the garden would be rather dull, as though someone had turned down the volume on my favorite movie. While it still might be lovely to watch, the wit and nuance of the true dialogue is lost. That being said, believe me when I say that owning chickens is not for the faint of heart. Should you want to raise them well and are even slightly concerned with cleanliness, chickens are an enormous amount of work.

When cities around the globe started allowing backyard chickens, many people embraced the idea. I think those who were considering it, myself included, figured how hard could it really be? All those happy urban chicken owners on Instagram make it look so easy. Just buy a little coop the size of a large dollhouse off Wayfair or Amazon and plunk it in the backyard, right? Unfortunately, I don't think the nice people at Wayfair have actually ever met a full-grown chicken, let alone three or four. Stuffing a bunch of chickens in a small, flimsy coop is a recipe for disaster. Just like humans, chickens can get nasty with each other if they feel crowded. Building a generous and solid all-season coop is crucial to everyone's happiness. It's important that the coop is sturdy and properly finished, which will make weekly cleanings much easier,

keep out drafts in the colder months, and deter sneaky rodents looking for a free meal.

Regardless of how nice a coop you have, though, the reality is chickens don't want to be confined all day. They want to roam and peck and scratch their way around your yard. If you have even an ounce of compassion and love for animals, once you witness how happy chickens are looking for worms on the front lawn or taking a dirt bath in the garden, you'll have a hard time locking them up for the day. But having your chickens roam free isn't the solution either. Besides the fact that left unattended they will eat your entire garden, chickens have many predators that are constantly on the hunt for snacks: eagles, dogs, raccoons, coyotes, and owls to name just a few.

Ideally, in addition to the coop, you will also have a fenced run for them to hang out in without the threat of attack. For those times you do let the ladies have a little run about, you'll want to stay with them and keep one eye to the sky, always on the lookout for bigger birds with even bigger appetites.

Then, without question, the one issue everyone seems to be shocked to discover is a chicken's annoying habit of merrily pooping on everything. It's a constant battle that there is no getting around. Without continual maintenance you'll quickly be forced to navigate your yard like a minefield if a hose isn't handy.

If you've read this far down the page and are more intrigued than horrified, chickens might be for you! I'm

sure you're wondering, if owning chickens is this much trouble why do I bother? Well, quite simply because I adore them. This wasn't always the case. There were definitely a few bumps in the beginning, but my chickens have trained me well, and at the end of the day, everyone is guilty of an appalling habit or two.

I imagine most people think the best part of keeping chickens is the constant supply of fresh eggs, and I'd be lying if I said I wasn't thrilled every time I find an egg in the nesting box. The quality and taste are without compare. Coco, my Cuckoo Maran, lays lovely dark brown eggs. Regina, my Ameraucana, lays the prettiest blue ones, and of course Olive, my Olive Egger, delivers shells in the most perfect shade of olive-green. The pride I feel every time I share them with friends is so over the top, you'd honestly think I'd laid them myself!

But as fantastic as the egg supply is, for me the best part of my life with chickens is witnessing their own happiness. Anyone who thinks chickens aren't intelligent and don't have feelings is clearly projecting. Chickens experience joy, express anger, and are very maternal. A mother hen is so dedicated to her chicks when sitting on a clutch of eggs, she will only step out once a day to get food or water. Chickens have an insatiable curiosity for life and feel deep sadness when they lose a friend. Just like people, every chicken has their own unique personality . . . some social, some bossy, some naughty, and some all of the above.

Chickens also have excellent memories and can recognize up to 100 faces, so you'd better behave when in their company because they won't forget you.

Sadly, chickens the world over generally have a horrible time of it. To keep costs down and egg production up, the living conditions for most factory laying birds are terrible. During their all-too-brief lives they rarely see the light of day, being kept stacked in wee cages under harsh fluorescent lighting. But I assure you, the first time you come upon a chicken deep into the pleasure of a dirt bath, rolling and cooing to her heart's content, or watch one seek out a sunny patch in the garden, lie down, and fan out her wings to bask in the warmth, you'll know why you keep chickens. Like

sharing Christmas morning with young children, just being the lucky spectator to such a pure and innocent joy makes sense of it all.

I recognize that raising chickens isn't an option for most people, but we can all do our part to try and buy eggs from reputable farms that raise their birds in a caring and humane environment. I encourage you to do some research on the brands offered in your grocery store or better yet, seek out a smaller local producer if possible.

The Language of Chickens

Flew the coop

Pecking order

Henpecked

Don't put all your eggs in one basket

Like a chicken with its head cut off

I'm no spring chicken

Egg on your face

Rule the roost

I can't read your chicken scratch

He's a bad egg

Scarce as hens' teeth

She's a mother hen

Don't count your chickens before they hatch

I've got a little nest egg

Ruffle your feathers

It's a chicken-and-egg situation

It will come home to roost

Feather your nest

Walking on eggshells

Shake a tail feather

There ain't nobody here but us chickens

SOME CHICKEN POINTERS

DO your homework! I did a lot of research in preparation for my chicks' arrival. I read everything I could get my hands on and spent a lot of time googling random questions. You can never be too prepared when raising a living creature! Some of my favorite reference books are *Keeping Chickens* by Jeremy Hobson and Celia Lewis, *The Beginner's Guide to Raising Chickens* by Anne Kuo, and *Backyard Farming: Raising Chickens* by Kim Pezza.

DO make sure to check your city bylaws before getting chickens to make sure it is allowed. Every city has its own rules, and you wouldn't want to make such an investment only to have a nosy neighbor turn you in.

DO consider all the different breeds when choosing your birds. There are so many options it will make your head spin. You'll need to think about what will work best for your specific situation. Some birds are better with children, some can withstand colder temperatures, and some will lay more eggs than others across a year. I chose my ladies based on the color of each of their eggshells rather than for looks and personality. As luck would have it, on top of the beautiful eggs they produce, they are also gorgeous with lovely dispositions. Of course, I may be slightly biased.

DO make sure you get at least three chickens. Chickens are meant to be part of a flock! A single chicken would be sad and lonely.

DON'T build the coop in direct sun. Chickens have a harder time with being too hot than too cold. Just make sure they have access to areas with sunshine so they can enjoy the heat as they choose.

DON'T feed your chickens anything moldy. Chickens love to eat scraps, which is helpful when cleaning up after breakfast or dinner, and as omnivores, they pretty much eat everything. But that doesn't mean old or expired food. It is also a good idea to print a list of specific foods that chickens can and can't eat and keep it handy so you can refer to it when in doubt.

DO make sure to consider the plant material around the yard where your chickens will be roaming, as some plants, such as foxglove, can be harmful if eaten.

DO make sure your chickens always have access to fresh, clean water all day long. Full-grown, laying hens drink about 2 cups/500 ml of water each per day and even more during the hot summer months.

DO make sure you always have a little dish of oyster shell and grit available to your chickens, as they need it to aid in their digestion and produce nice hard shells.

DO remember that you only need to refrigerate eggs if you have washed them. A fresh eggshell is covered in a "bloom" or "cuticle," a natural coating that keeps air and bacteria out of the egg. Fresh eggs that haven't been rinsed will keep nicely on the kitchen counter for several weeks. You can give them a rinse under warm water before cracking them open.

Cleaning the Coop

I like to give the coop a proper cleaning once a week. This might seem like a lot to some, but I find if I stay on top of it, the job doesn't take long. If I only cleaned the coop once a month, it would be a much bigger, messier chore. When designing the coop, I gave a lot of consideration to the materials used to try and make the maintenance as easy as possible. I chose to paint the whole interior with a washable latex and then had vinyl plank flooring installed. The flooring is waterproof and scratch resistant, which makes cleanup a breeze. Like most things in life, once you have a system in place, things go much more smoothly. In an effort to give you a little jump-start, here is a step by step on how I tackle the task.

1. Thoroughly sweep out all litter and waste. I prefer to use pine shavings for my girls, but straw, hay, or shredded paper are good alternatives.

2. I put the shavings in a large paper leaf bag and dispose of it in our green waste bin.

3. Remove any water or pellet feeders from the coop. Wash and dry all feeders and refill them with fresh pellets and water.

4. Fill a big mop bucket with hot soapy water. I use both a cleaning cloth and a mop with a removable head. That way I can toss it all in the washing machine when I'm done cleaning. Wipe down the walls, nesting boxes, and roosting bars and then mop all the floors. I use a spray bottle with a multi-surface cleaner to spray the floors before mopping.

5. I take extra care with the corners and crevices, as this is where annoying bugs like to hide.

6. Dust the inside of the coop with a food-grade diatomaceous earth, a natural and organic insecticide. I encourage you to buy a powder duster to make the application much easier. They retail for $10 to $20 but are worth every penny.

7. Fill the coop and nesting boxes with fresh pine shavings and then sprinkle with Nesting Box Potpourri (see page 214). Place the refilled feeders back inside. As a final step, I always give a little sweep around the outside of the coop because somehow the pine shavings manage to escape.

That's it! Good as new! (Until next week.)

NESTING BOX POTPOURRI

Nothing makes me and my ladies happier than a freshly cleaned coop! A clean living space is integral to the overall health of your birds. Left to their own devices, things could get smelly pretty quickly.

I love sprinkling this herbal blend around the coop as a last step. I'm not sure whether the chickens appreciate the extra effort, but I like to think they do. I order all the ingredients off Amazon, make up a big batch, and store it in ziplock bags; it will last for months and months. The mint, wormwood, and tansy help deter bugs, and the scent of lavender, chamomile, and calendula is very calming.

Dried lavender

Dried tansy

Dried spearmint

Dried calendula petals

Dried wormwood

Dried rose petals

Dried rosemary

Dried raspberry leaf

Dried chamomile

There are no specific measurements or instructions to follow. I simply combine one bag each of the above ingredients, with each bag being about 3½ oz/100 g.

COCO, OLIVE & REGINA'S SPECIAL SCRATCH BLEND

There is nothing chickens love more than scratching around the ground looking for snacks! They're always on the hunt for insects, grass, and grit. While it's important not to indulge your birds with extra goodies too often, a handful of scratch tossed on the lawn or in the run is a source of great entertainment and makes for very happy birds!

You can buy ready-made scratch, but I find it to be rather pricey compared to making my own. Just like my Nesting Box Potpourri, all the ingredients can be purchased easily online. I store the scratch in a small garbage can with a lockable lid to prevent greedy squirrels and rodents from breaking in.

Organic oat groats

Organic wheat

Organic shelled sunflower seeds

Organic pumpkin seeds

Organic pearl barley

Cracked corn

Dried mealworms

A combination of these ingredients makes for great scratch that no chicken could refuse. Simply combine equal parts or as close to equal as you can. If the cracked corn comes in a bigger bag than the other ingredients, so be it. Your chickens won't complain and if they do, you won't understand a word they're saying.

THE FLOWERS

INGREDIENTS FOR A COTTAGE GARDEN

Without question, my favorite part of any garden is the flowers. While I appreciate the fruit and vegetables that I grow for nourishing my body, it is the flowers that feed my heart and soul.

There are many different styles and approaches to creating a garden, but I will always be drawn to the humble charm of an English cottage garden. There is something about a jumble of plants and flowers billowing from old pots and spilling onto paths that makes me smile and relax. Its casual beauty feels unplanned and joyful, like a toddler climbing out of bed in the morning with their jammies rumpled and their hair askew, ready to greet the day with a pure, infectious happiness that is hard to resist.

Just as a wine store can be a little daunting to the average shopper, so can a nursery to a novice gardener. With so much to choose from, where does one start? I've put together a list of my tried-and-true, can't-live-without-them flowers and their specific varieties that I love for my garden, BUT believe me when I tell you that I've barely scratched the surface on the endless choices out there. Like everything in life, it's all about an education. The more you read, the more you grow, and the more questions you ask, the more adventurous and confident you will become with your selections.

When shopping for plants, it's important to note the distinction between perennials and annuals. Annual plants grow for only one season and die off at the first hard frost, whereas perennials, under the same conditions, only die off what grows above ground. Below the surface they are as happy as can be and will return, bigger and better, the following spring and for years to come. Perennials make up much of my garden, but because their bloom time isn't always that long, I love to fill out the rest of the beds and pots with showy annuals that offer flowers throughout the summer months. Cosmos, sweet peas, and nasturtiums are just a few of the annuals that can add lovely color to your garden for many weeks. Just remember to pinch off or "deadhead" any old blooms daily and fertilize at least once a month for a continued show.

One of your greatest resources when out shopping for plants will be the little tag tucked inside every plant pot at the nursery. These tags offer a wealth of information about the plant, including its habits, bloom time, height, spacing, and light requirements. I have a box in my greenhouse where I keep all the tags from my plant purchases. They make a terrific reference should anyone ask about a plant in my garden that I can't remember the name of and serve as a little scrapbook of things that worked or sadly didn't.

The single most important task when taking care of any garden, especially a cutting garden, must be watering. A proper watering of your plants is vital to their health and survival! By proper, I mean a really good soaking, not a weak, lazy sprinkle over top. It's best to water in the early morning or late evening when the soil is cooler and less prone to evaporation. I prefer to hand water my flower beds and pots to make sure I'm delivering a big drink right to the roots instead of soaking the leaves. Wet leaves in the evening can lead to mildew, and water left on leaves in the heat of the day acts like little magnifying glasses for the sun, which can cause burn marks to develop.

If you are planting taller plants like dahlias, hollyhocks, or delphiniums, it's a good idea to start staking them right from the get-go even though it might seem unnecessary. You can make adjustments as they grow and even replace the early stakes with stronger, taller ones if need be, which is much easier to do than trying to wrangle a four-foot dahlia that has flopped over because of a heavy rain or the weight of a really big bloom.

Perennials

BEEBLOSSOM (*Gaura lindheimeri*)
   Whirling Butterflies
A lovely plant with fine, wiry stems laden with little white blooms tinged with pale pink. It likes full sun and good drainage but all in all is pretty easy to care for.

BELLFLOWER (*Campanula carpatica*)
   White Clips
   Deep Blue Clips
This plant grows in nice mounds, throwing up stems of white or purple bell-shaped flowers. It does fine in full sun to partial shade, but given its invasive habit, I like to contain it by tucking it in my planters.

CATMINT (*Nepeta racemosa*)
   Walker's Low
   Little Titch
One of my all-time favorite plants. I love the way *Nepeta* billows from planters or spills onto the pathways, softening all the hard edges. Once its initial bloom is over, you can cut the whole plant back and it will do it all over again! It is happy in full sun to partial shade.

CLEMATIS (*Clematis*)
   Empress
   Apple Blossom
I am not a fan of most clematis, as I find they can look a little scraggly when not in bloom, but when their flowers show up it all makes sense. The first year I planted my Empress clematis it was so unimpressive I was very close to ripping it out! Luckily, I never got around to it, and it now puts on the most spectacular show every spring, with little or no effort on my part. Find a sunny wall and be patient; it will be worth it.

COLUMBINE (*Aquilegia vulgaris*)
   Clementine Salmon Rose
A very hardy perennial that is easy to grow. There are lots of varieties of columbine, but I love this particular one for its graceful stems laden with the prettiest pink double flowers. It does best in partial shade.

CREEPING JENNY (*Lysimachia nummularia*)
The name may conjure up some strange images, but it is a nice, low-growing perennial that makes a pretty carpet of shiny leaves. Unless of course your chickens discover it; then it won't do much at all. I like to use it tucked into planters where it will grow over the edge and hang down. It is happy in full sun to partial shade.

DELPHINIUM (*Delphinium elatum*)
   Guardian Lavender
   Highlander Moon Light
That tall, good-looking friend we all have. The one that stands out in a crowd. Yep, that's a delphinium. Beautiful in a border and will bloom all summer in full sun or partial shade.

EUPHORBIA (*Euphorbia characias* subsp. *wulfenii*)
   Mediterranean Spurge
I love the bold structure a euphorbia provides in the garden. With its bluish-green evergreen leaves, contrasted in the spring with large, bright lime-green blooms, it makes the perfect counterpart to dainty flowers like cosmos or tickseed. It is happiest in full sun.

GERANIUM (*Pelargonium*)
Horizon Apple Blossom

A classic that works in the yard all season long and then sits happily on a sunny windowsill indoors for the winter months.

HYDRANGEA (*Hydrangea paniculata*)
Limelight

Most hydrangeas prefer shade, but the Limelight has no problem with full sun. They grow quite large so best to plant it towards the back of the bed. It has lovely big blooms that make beautiful arrangements, either fresh or dried.

HYDRANGEA (*Hydrangea macrophylla*)
Onyx Flamingo

I love this hydrangea for the loads of pale pink mophead blooms it provides in both the garden and vases throughout the house. It does best in partial shade but will tolerate the sun as long as the soil is kept moist.

IRON CROSS SHAMROCK (*Oxalis tetraphylla*)

A lot of gardeners will steer you away from *Oxalis* because of its invasive tendencies, but this variety is not invasive. I love it for its pretty heart-shaped leaves that are the perfect shade of green with a dark purple marking at the base. Throughout the summer months, the leaves are topped with small, bright-pink blooms. They are said to tolerate full sun but appear to be happiest in my garden in partial shade.

JAPANESE ANEMONE (*Anemone hupehensis*)
Queen Charlotte

We have a big patch of this plant growing beside the driveway, and I look forward to it blooming every year. It produces hundreds of the prettiest pale pink flowers on long, willowy stems perfect for cutting. It blooms later in the summer right through the beginning of fall and is happy in full sun or partial shade.

LADY'S-MANTLE (*Alchemilla mollis*)
Thriller

No garden is complete without at least one good patch of lady's-mantle. It's the perfect edge to a path or border with its mounds of green leaves, so soft they have an almost suede-like finish. The tip of each leaf is perfectly scalloped, which catches the morning dew or a light rain beautifully, creating a magical crown-like effect. Make sure to head out to the garden early in the morning so you don't miss it. This plant will tolerate full sun but is happiest in something a little more dappled.

LAMB'S EARS (*Stachys byzantina*)
Big Ears

No one can resist touching this plant! The silvery-green leaves are covered in a soft fuzz that feels like velvet . . . or I imagine a lamb's ear. Plant this one for the lovely foliage, not the blooms, and make sure it has full sun.

LAVENDER (*Lavandula*)
Fred Boutin

Of all the different kinds of lavender, I prefer this one for its long, elegant stems over the low, tight clumps of other more commonly recognized varieties. This plant will bloom in mid to late summer and needs lots of sunshine to thrive.

MEXICAN FLEABANE (*Erigeron karvinskianus*)
Profusion

Erigeron is my weakness, and I will never have enough in my garden. I love the way it masses and trails over walkways or planters, providing an endless show of wee little pink and white daisies. It can sometimes prove difficult to find at the nursery, but I have had great success growing it from seed in the early spring. I order the seeds through Chiltern Seeds in the UK (see the source guide for contact information). *Erigeron* is another sun lover.

PEONY (*Paeonia*)
 Coral Charm

The peony . . . Instagram's favorite flower! One of the
first flowers to bloom in the garden and a true sign that
summer is beginning. They make beautiful cut flowers
of a deep coral color when they first open, slowly fading
to palest creamy yellow the fuller they become. Peonies
are happy in full sun to partial shade but don't like to be
moved, so pick their home carefully and leave them be.

PINCUSHION FLOWER (*Scabiosa atropurpurea*)
 Butterfly Blue
 Snow Maiden
 Salmon Queen

I seem to have a real attraction to flowers that grow on
long, wiry stems. Maybe it's because I wish I had long,
wiry stems but let's not start to try and unpack that
right now. *Scabiosa* have the prettiest flowers, each with
a cushion-like center covered in wee stems, looking
much like the name suggests. They are easy to care for
and will continue to produce all summer long with lots
of sunshine and regular deadheading.

ROSES (*Rosa*)
 Dylan
 Golden Opportunity
 Cecile Brunner
 Bathsheba
 Koko Loko

My love of roses could fill its own volume, so it was
hard making this list! These are, however, some of my
very favorites, with the Dylan rose ranking number one
for its lovely baby-pink blooms. When choosing your
roses, just make sure to select ones that have healthy,
hardy leaves with no signs of disease and strong stems.
Plant them in the sunniest spot you have and make sure
to fertilize every 2 to 3 weeks throughout the summer
months to keep those blooms coming!

SALVIA (*Salvia nemorosa*)
 Crystal Blue

A really nice upright perennial with flowering spikes of
a pretty, icy blue. I am a big fan of this low-maintenance
plant and so are the honeybees and butterflies. Salvia
likes the sun but is also drought tolerant so doesn't
require as much water as most of the other plants listed.

SUN ROSE/ROCK ROSE (*Helianthemum nummularium*)
 Cheviot

I love this little, low-growing evergreen shrub for the
abundance of delicate peachy-pink flowers it produces.
Each flower opens for only 1 day, but not to worry:
there are always plenty more buds in the queue, making
a wonderful show for months. It works beautifully in
my pots and planters but is also a lovely ground cover
for a sunny patch.

TICKSEED (*Coreopsis*)
 Shades of Rose
 Big Bang Mercury Rising
 Big Bang Star Cluster

Coreopsis is a recent discovery for me and an instant
favorite, hence the three different varieties I listed! It is
another lovely plant with fine stems that will continually
produce masses of flowers all season long if you remember
to deadhead every day. I like to plant mine in pots so
that they can be easily moved about the garden to create
new vignettes. *Coreopsis* is another sun lover.

VIOLA (*Viola cornuta*)
 Lilac Ice
 Antique Shades
 Arkwright Ruby

I am a little obsessed with violas. Much like *Erigeron*,
I'd happily plant it in every container and bed in my
garden. Don't underestimate this small, dainty plant as
it has an amazing work ethic, producing an abundance
of blooms from early spring right through late fall. A
spot in partial shade and daily deadheading will ensure
continual supply all summer long.

Annuals

CHINA ASTER (*Callistephus chinensis*)
    Matsumoto Apricot
Produces sweet little pale-peach flowers on long stems
that make a perfect addition to any bouquet.

CHOCOLATE COSMOS (*Cosmos atrosanguineus*)
Its blooms aren't just the color of chocolate, it also has
the scent of chocolate! So again, chocolate proves to
be awesome.

COSMOS (*Cosmos bipinnatus*)
    Sonata White
    Apricot Lemonade
I love big pots on the patio filled with cosmos. I make
a point to go out every evening before watering the
garden and use a small pair of snips to remove any tired
blooms. It takes only a minute, and by morning a whole
new crop will have opened.

DAHLIA
    Sweet Nathalie
    Apple Blossom
    Polka
    Linda's Baby
    Penhill Watermelon
    Snoho Doris
    Breakout
    Jowey Winnie
Dahlias are grown from tubers, so they are not
technically an annual. Should you carefully dig them up
in the fall and store them safely, you can definitely
replant them every spring. If you don't find the time for
this step, just remember that the dahlia plant, having
originated in Mexico, won't survive once the temperature drops below freezing. Dahlias have become a real
passion for me, and I look forward to growing them
every year. But they have also become a lot of other
people's passion too, and purchasing tubers can prove
to be challenging. Online sales have become very
competitive and sell out in a matter of moments. I have

included some of my favorite suppliers in the resource list, so pay close attention to when their annual sales start if you too would like to go dahlia-crazy.

DOUBLE HOLLYHOCK (*Alcea rosea*)
Peaches 'n' Dreams
Fiesta Time

I love the drama of a really tall hollyhock. It is hard to imagine that one tiny little seed could produce something like that! Peaches 'n' Dreams has spectacular double blooms in the prettiest shade of pale salmon. Both hollyhocks and foxgloves (see below) are actually biennial, meaning they produce only roots and leaves in the first year of planting, bloom the second year, and then die. This is why I categorize them as annuals. I prefer to purchase them as small plants in their second year from the nursery so that I can enjoy the flowers without the long wait.

FOXGLOVE (*Digitalis purpurea*)
Dalmatian Peach
Arctic Fox Rose

My garden would never be complete without foxgloves, though I am selective about where I plant them as they can be toxic to animals. I plant foxgloves in higher planters and pots so my chickens avoid them. Foxgloves are happy in partial shade. Foxgloves are actually biennials; read more above, under Double Hollyhock.

LEMON SCENTED GERANIUM (*Pelargonium citronellum*)
Mabel Grey

The leaves of this plant have the most wonderful scent, just as the name suggests. It also has a robust growing habit, so I don't hesitate to cut it when making floral arrangements for the house.

NASTURTIUM (*Tropaeolum*)
Cherry Rose Jewel
Yeti
Whirlybird Rose

Unlike the standard orange nasturtium that is more commonly known, these varieties are in shades of deep pink and soft creamy yellow. Nasturtiums love to trail, so plant them at the edge of a big pot or hanging basket for a dramatic show and remember to use their edible leaves and flowers in salads or as a pretty garnish on any dish.

SILVER FALLS (*Dichondra*)

Every season I like to buy a flat of *Dichondra* to underplant some of my flowers in pots. Before long masses of silver leaves are trailing like waterfalls around the garden. *Dichondra* is actually a perennial, but because I like to switch up plant combinations in my pots from year to year, I generally treat it as an annual.

SWEET PEAS (*Lathyrus odoratus*)
Mollie Rilstone
Charlie's Angels
Earl Grey
Memorial Flight

Is there anything nicer than the scent of a sweet pea? People take a lot of pride in growing sweet peas, myself included. Early in the spring, I start my sweet peas from seed, searching out the prettiest varieties in a range of pastels. Sweet peas need to climb but have very tender tendrils. Make sure they have full sun and fine netting or string them on a trellis they can grab as they grow.

TWINSPUR (*Diascia*)
My Darling Peach

A pretty, frothy annual with delicate little blooms. It is lovely tucked in with other plants, but I also love it on its own in a single pot. It likes full sun but will also tolerate a little shade.

FORAGING & ARRANGING

I am definitely the kind of woman who has a pair of sharp clippers in her glove box at all times. You just never know when you might come upon a patch of wildflowers growing by the side of the road, so I like to be prepared. Now just to be clear, I am not suggesting you raid your neighbor's garden bed for your next bouquet, but should the branches of a random lilac bush be hanging over a fence and calling your name, go ahead and cut yourself a few. If you discover a patch of poppies that have self-seeded in the back lane on your next dog walk, don't hesitate to snip, snip, snip. You'll be amazed by what is growing all around you if you keep your eyes open.

We are fortunate to live very close to some beautiful walking trails along the riverside. Every spring I patiently wait for the cow parsley to come into bloom. For a brief period, the roadsides and wooded paths are overflowing with its delicate white flowers. I make a point to never let the moment pass without pulling my car over at least once. I take out those clippers and set about filling my trunk with a big bundle, all free for the taking, and then rush home to create a show-stopping arrangement.

Flowers will never last as long in a vase as they will in the garden, but I am a firm believer in enjoying the flowers I grow and sharing them with friends. It is called a cutting garden after all.

Many flowers, including sweet peas, dahlias, cosmos, and zinnias, even benefit from being cut.

They fall into the "cut and come again" category, which, just as the name suggests, means that the very act of cutting a bloom encourages the plant to produce another. It really is the gift that keeps on giving.

I always make sure to add a teaspoon of bleach to the water before placing the flowers in their chosen vessel. The bleach helps prevent bacteria from growing and keeps the stems from getting slimy, which can make water absorption difficult and the water smell rather nasty. On that front, I make sure to check the water level daily and freshen it as necessary. It's also important when trimming stems to first remove any leaves that fall below the water line. Always use a sharp, clean knife or clippers and cut the stems on a 45-degree angle. This will help to maximize the exposed area to water, making it easier for thirsty flowers to drink. It also allows the stems to stand on a point instead of a blunt edge, much like being on your tippy toes versus standing flat-footed, which could block the access to water.

My floral-arranging skills are rather limited, but I can't go too far wrong when working with the lovely flowers that grow in my garden. I try not to overthink things when arranging flowers or I find myself second-guessing my efforts. Instead, I hope to present them as I would find them in the garden; simple, relaxed, and natural.

Fortunately, I'm not one for intricate bouquets; I much prefer the simplicity of showcasing just one kind of flower without the distraction of a lot of filler. I love a mass of roses or dahlias placed in a vintage pitcher or

the striking elegance of delphiniums in a tall glass vase. A generous handful of sweet peas or cosmos look completely at home in an old marmalade jar or tin mug perched beside the kitchen sink. But for all the beauty that kind of fullness can offer, I am always pleasantly surprised by how impactful a single stem, or even a grouping of vases with one stem in each, can be. Five or seven foxgloves in bud vases running down the middle of a table or a few dainty stems of chocolate cosmos in teeny-tiny old medicine bottles can pack quite a visual punch for very little effort.

It is also important to consider the space you plan to place your flowers. A wild and woolly bouquet might look amazing on the dinner table during the day but could prove to be rather impractical come mealtime—as could anything highly fragrant, such as hyacinth or lilac, which can be overpowering when eating. Either of those same arrangements, though, could be wonderful in a front entrance, both for scale and the pleasure of being greeted with a beautiful scent upon entering your home. A smaller posy or a singular stem will showcase a little better in a more intimate space, like on a bedside table, in a powder room, or beside the kitchen sink. This allows you to experience and appreciate their beauty up close, whereas the dainty stems could be lost in a larger open space. On the other hand, I like to save taller and bolder arrangements for spots that can be viewed from a distance to fully appreciate their structure and height. I love the way a large urn full of cherry blossom branches or a massive bundle of forsythia creates a dramatic focal point that is both whimsical and fresh, as though I have truly brought the outdoors in.

SOURCE GUIDE

Fence & Planter Construction

LOU MAYER FENCING
If you live in the Vancouver area and you need a new fence, Lou is the man.
1-604-765-0702

Greenhouse Supply

BC GREENHOUSE BUILDERS
I couldn't love my greenhouse more and highly recommend this company if you are considering getting one.
www.bcgreenhouses.com

Stonework, Stone & Pea Gravel

ROCK SOLID STONEWORKS
Mark doesn't have a website or use social media to promote his work . . . he doesn't need to. He is that good!
1-604-861-8182

ADERA NATURAL STONE SUPPLY
Wonderful resource for all things stone.
www.aderastone.com

NORTHWEST LANDSCAPE & STONE SUPPLY
They have it all here . . . from stone to pots to water feature supplies.
www.landscapesupply.com

LAWNBOY GARDEN & LANDSCAPE SUPPLY
My pea gravel and soil dealers. Don't worry, they deliver.
www.lawnboylandscape.com

Paint & Stain Supply

BENJAMIN MOORE PAINT & STAIN
I have ordered so many cans of solid stain in Amherst Gray I have now lost count.
www.benjaminmoore.com

Vintage Planters & Pots

ETSY
My favorite resource for pretty much anything you can think of.
www.etsy.com

SOUTHLANDS NURSERY
My friend Tom has the BEST nursery around, and besides all the beautiful plants he carries, he also always has an amazing selection of vintage, antique, and reproduction planters, urns, and statuary.
www.southlandsnursery.com

SCOTT LANDON ANTIQUES
Scott has a great eye, and I have found some lovely old pieces on his site.
www.scottlandonantiques.com

Gardening Tools

GARDEN AND WOOD
A wonderful resource for refurbished garden tools that not only work perfectly but look amazing too!
www.gardenandwood.co.uk

GARDENER'S KIT
A wonderful shop with locations in both Vancouver and in Victoria, BC, that sells a wide selection of Japanese hand tools, ladders, plant supports, and the Sneeboer range of tools. They have a great online shop.
www.gardenerskit.com

My Favorite Nurseries

SOUTHLANDS NURSERY
The best part about the home we live in is how close it is to this nursery. Being only a 3-minute drive down the hill, during the spring and summer I seem to find a reason to pop down every day, much to Paul's dismay.
www.southlandsnursery.com

CEDAR RIM NURSERY
A much farther drive for me but always worth it.
www.cedarrim.com

WESTERN INDEPENDENT GREENHOUSES
A great nursery with great prices.
www.wigplants.com

SELECT ROSES
Brad Jalbert is the rose man and is recognized far and wide as such. He stocks the most beautiful roses, but be warned . . . they sell out quickly. To get the best selection, I always place my order online in the fall and pick up the following spring when they're ready to plant. His website also has lots of wonderful information about caring for roses.
www.selectroses.ca

PETERSHAM NURSERIES
One of my favorite places on earth and a true inspiration for any gardener. Located in Richmond, just outside London, I make a point to visit whenever I am nearby. I bought my favorite old watering can from them and carried it home on the plane!
www.petershamnurseries.com

BURFORD GARDEN CO.
Also located in England, it must be seen to be believed. This is so much more than a nursery or garden center . . . more of a garden world. If you find yourself in Burford, make sure to stop in as they presently don't ship outside the UK.
www.burford.co.uk

Seeds & Dahlia Tubers

JOHNNY'S SELECTED SEEDS
Johnny's has an excellent selection of seeds for vegetables and flowers.
www.johnnyseeds.com

FLORET FLOWERS
Anyone who loves flowers, loves Floret. Their seed sales sell out quickly, so organize your selection beforehand.
www.floretflowers.com

CHILTERN SEEDS
If you are hunting for *Erigeron* seeds and lovely sweet peas, this is the place!
www.chilternseeds.co.uk

BAKER CREEK HEIRLOOM SEEDS
My go-to spot for beautiful viola seeds.
www.rareseeds.com

Dahlia tuber shopping is an intense thing . . . like trying to snag tickets to a popular show on Broadway. Here is a list of some of my favorite growers . . . good luck!
www.coseytownflowers.com
www.stonemeadowgardens.ca
www.thedahliaexpert.ca
www.manygraces.com
www.brecksbulbs.ca
www.creeksidegrowers.ca

Antique Dishes & Serving Pieces

ETSY
Some people read the paper over breakfast. I'd rather check in with Etsy.
www.etsy.com

ELSIE GREEN
Another wonderful source for all things vintage.
www.elsiegreen.com

Table Linens

BACCI'S
A wonderful spot for lovely housewares and more!
www.baccisvancouver.com

CUTTER BROOKS
A beautiful shop located in the Cotswolds, but fortunately they ship worldwide. You can find an excellent selection of tableware and linens online.
www.cutterbrooks.com

THE CROSS
Another gorgeous shop filled with everything one could want for their home.
www.thecrossdesign.com

Flowers

QUINCE FINE FLORALS
Just in case you don't have a cutting garden of your own. Jessica is a dear friend and wonderful florist.
www.quincefineflorals.com

Chicken Things

BUCKERFIELD'S
If you're looking to purchase baby chicks, this is the spot!
www.buckerfields.ca

KLASSEN WOOD CO.
I use pine shavings in the coop, and my girls think Klassen has the cleanest, softest ones ever!
www.klassenwoodco.com

ROYAL ROOSTER

I think this company makes the best chicken feeders. Very streamlined and attractive plus easy to install and clean.

www.royal-rooster.com

AMAZON

My go-to source for all the ingredients for my chicken scratch and herbal nesting box potpourri.

www.amazon.ca
www.amazon.com
www.amazon.co.uk

Garden Clothes & Shoes

FOG LINEN

I live in their aprons! My favorite is the Square Cross in natural; it's super roomy with a pocket for your keys or phone.

www.shop-foglinen.com

HUNTER

I am very attached to my gardening clogs.

www.hunterboots.com

Garden Maps

Should you want a beautiful hand-painted garden map (or an illustrator for any other purpose) Wendy Nooney, the illustrator of my garden map on page 10, is the best.

www.nooneyart.com

Farmers' Markets

Just in case you don't have the space or time to grow your own vegetables, your local farmers' market will be able to provide everything you need. These are some of my personal favorites. Even when I am traveling, nothing makes me happier than coming upon a farmers' market. I can't lug all that beautiful produce home, but it is still an absolute joy to walk the aisles and admire the bounty!

VANCOUVER MARKETS

www.eatlocal.org
www.ubcfarm.ubc.ca

NEW YORK

www.grownyc.org

LOS ANGELES

www.farmersmarketla.com

LONDON

www.lfm.org.uk

You Say Tomahto and I Say Tomayto

To make sure we are all on the same page, I thought it might be helpful to create a little cheat sheet for various vegetables, ingredients, tools, and techniques, in case you're reading this from outside North America.

All-purpose flour—plain flour

Appetizer—starter

Arugula—rocket

Bacon—rasher/streaky bacon

Baking soda—bicarbonate of soda

Beet—Beetroot

Broil—grill

Butter lettuce—round lettuce

Chickpea—garbanzo

Cilantro—coriander

Cookie—biscuit

Dark brown sugar—muscovado sugar

Dessert—pudding

Eggplant—aubergine

Golden raisin—sultana

Granulated sugar—castor sugar

Green beans—French beans

Green onion—spring onion

Ground meat—mince

Ham—gammon

Icing (powdered) sugar—confectioners' sugar

Jam—jelly

Napa cabbage—winter cabbage

Parchment paper—baking paper

Pastry flour—cake flour

Plastic wrap—cling film

Prawn—shrimp

Red pepper—red bell pepper

Salad greens—salad leaves

Shredded coconut—desiccated coconut

Whipping cream—double cream

A HEARTFELT THANK YOU

To Paul, for always saying yes to my ideas even if it means you'll have to shovel an enormous amount of pea gravel. I love our garden but not as much as I love you.

To India, where would I even begin to thank you? IT services, taxi driver, recipe prep, lunch runs, Airbnb host, grammar checker, and soooo much more . . . you did it all and kept me sane and laughing. I love you more than words can say.

To Leon, I can't imagine what my home or my life would look like without you, and I hope I never have to. Thank you for not getting mad every time I call and ask you to make the chicken fence higher.

To Lou and Byron, no one builds a finer fence (or planter box or chicken run or tool shed . . .) than the two of you!

To Tony, there would be no side garden without water, and there would be no water without you. Thank you for installing the hose bib and thank you for fixing it every winter. I promise to remember to turn the hose off this year . . . this time for sure.

To Cam, thank you for teaching Paul the stonemason way.

To Bacci, thank you for making my panna cotta look so good!

To Damen, thank you for your kindness, patience, and perfect eye. You've helped me make sense of it all, and for that I am so grateful.

To Gord, thank you for building my girls the most beautiful and solid home. They are the envy of all their chicken friends!

To Tom, thank you for your wonderful nursery filled to the brim with all my favorite things and for generously lending me so many of your treasures. You being located all of 5 minutes from my front door is possibly the greatest or most dangerous thing in my life.

To Mum, thank you for always sharing your roses with me. I hope mine are as nice as yours one day.

To Lolita, your love of my garden is the greatest compliment I could receive. Thank you for your friendship and guidance.

To Oscar, thank you for being so bloody strong (good riddance to bamboo).

To Jessica, there is no one I'd rather swap seeds with. If gardeners needed a partner in crime, you'd be mine.

To Claire, you'll always be my favorite sous-chef.

To Andrew, thank you for the bravery you showed in getting on a plane to travel across the pond and work with a lady you'd never met. You have made this book everything I dreamed it could be and more. For all the bad things one can say about social media, once in a while, it gets it right.

To Robert and Lindsay, I can't believe this is the fourth time I get to thank you in print! I'm so grateful you could see what I see when you step into my garden. Thank you for trusting my vision and giving me the opportunity to share it with others. Hopefully our book will inspire people to get outside and make the world a little more beautiful.

INDEX

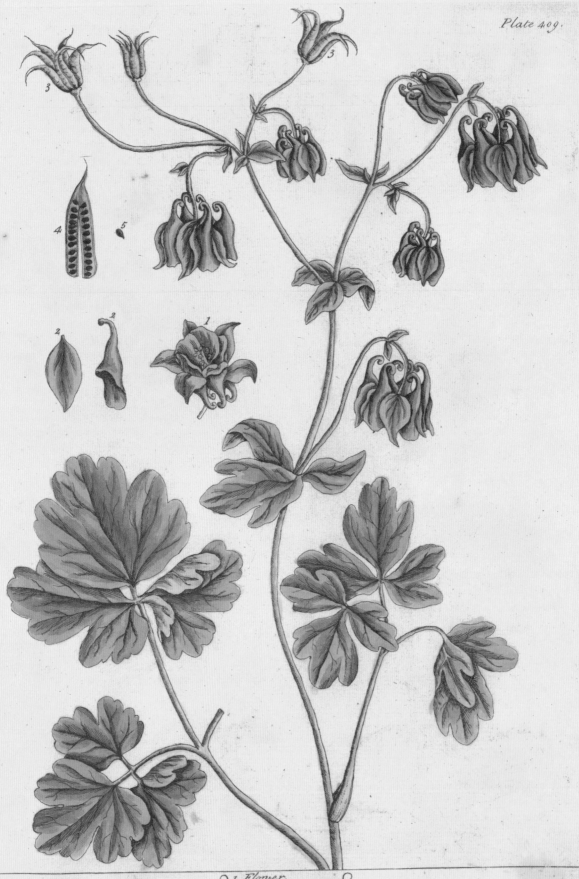

Plate 409.

Columbine

Aquilegia.

1. Flower.
2. Flower separate.
3. Seed Vessel.
4. Seed Vessel open.
5. Seed.

Eliz. Blackwell delin. sculp. et Pinx.